THE CREATIVE TAROT

✦✦✦✦✦━━━✦✦✦✦✦

A MODERN GUIDE TO AN INSPIRED LIFE

JESSA CRISPIN

Touchstone

New York   London   Toronto   Sydney   New Delhi

Touchstone
An Imprint of Simon & Schuster, Inc.
1230 Avenue of the Americas
New York, NY 10020

First Touchstone trade paperback edition February 2016

TOUCHSTONE and colophon are registered trademarks of
Simon & Schuster, Inc.

For information about special discounts for bulk purchases,
please contact Simon & Schuster Special Sales at 1-866-506-1949
or business@simonandschuster.com.

The Simon & Schuster Speakers Bureau can bring authors to your
live event. For more information or to book an event, contact the
Simon & Schuster Speakers Bureau at 1-866-248-3049 or visit our
website at www.simonspeakers.com.

Interior design by Jill Putorti
Spolia artwork by Jen May

Manufactured in the United States of America

10   9   8   7   6   5

Library of Congress Cataloging-in-Publication Data

Names: Crispin, Jessa.
Title: The creative tarot : a modern guide to an inspired life / Jessa Crispin.
Description: First Touchstone trade paperback edition. | New York : Touchstone, 2016.
Identifiers: LCCN 2015038927
Subjects: LCSH: Tarot. | Creative ability—Miscellanea.
Classification: LCC BF1879.T2 C695 2016 | DDC 133.3/2424—dc23
LC record available at http://lccn.loc.gov/2015038927

ISBN 978-1-5011-2023-7
ISBN 978-1-5011-2024-4 (ebook)

For Llorraine, Wendy, Jen, and all of
the other witchy women in my life

CONTENTS

Introduction   xi

A History of the Tarot   1
   A History of Artists and Tarot   10
   My Own History with the Tarot   20

The Cards   27
   Major Arcana   27
   Minor Arcana   27
   Swords   28
   Cups   28
   Wands   28
   Coins   29
   Court Cards   29

The Fool   33

The Magician   36

The High Priestess   39

The Empress   42

The Emperor   45

The Hierophant   48

The Lovers   51

The Chariot   54

Strength   57

The Hermit   60

The Wheel of Fortune   63

CONTENTS

Justice   66

The Hanged Man   69

Death   73

Temperance   76

The Devil   79

The Tower   82

The Star   85

The Moon   88

The Sun   91

Judgment   94

The World   97

The Aces   100
  Ace of Swords   102
  Ace of Cups   104
  Ace of Wands   107
  Ace of Coins   109

The Twos   111
  Two of Swords   113
  Two of Cups   116
  Two of Wands   119
  Two of Coins   121

The Threes   124
  Three of Swords   126
  Three of Cups   128
  Three of Wands   131
  Three of Coins   134

The Fours   136
  Four of Swords   138
  Four of Cups   141
  Four of Wands   144
  Four of Coins   147

CONTENTS

The Fives   150
    Five of Swords   152
    Five of Cups   155
    Five of Wands   158
    Five of Coins   161

The Sixes   164
    Six of Swords   166
    Six of Cups   169
    Six of Wands   171
    Six of Coins   174

The Sevens   177
    Seven of Swords   179
    Seven of Cups   182
    Seven of Wands   184
    Seven of Coins   187

The Eights   189
    Eight of Swords   191
    Eight of Cups   194
    Eight of Wands   196
    Eight of Coins   198

The Nines   201
    Nine of Swords   203
    Nine of Cups   206
    Nine of Wands   208
    Nine of Coins   211

The Tens   213
    Ten of Swords   215
    Ten of Cups   218
    Ten of Wands   220
    Ten of Coins   222

The Pages   225
    Page of Swords   227
    Page of Cups   230
    Page of Wands   233
    Page of Coins   236

CONTENTS

The Knights   238
   Knight of Swords   240
   Knight of Cups   243
   Knight of Wands   246
   Knight of Coins   249

The Queens   252
   Queen of Swords   255
   Queen of Cups   258
   Queen of Wands   261
   Queen of Coins   264

The Kings   267
   King of Swords   269
   King of Cups   272
   King of Wands   275
   King of Coins   278

The Spreads   281
   Finding Inspiration   285
   Sample Reading   287
   The Creative Block   288
   Sample Reading   292
   Creating Structure   294
   Sample Reading   295
   Checking Your Direction   296
   Sample Reading   299
   Bringing Your Project into the World   301
   Sample Reading   304
   Conclusion   307

How to Do a Reading   309
   The Setup   309
   Get to Know the Cards   310
   Choose a Deck   313
   Find the Patterns   314
   Tell a Story   319
   How to Read for Someone Else   322
   Keep a Journal   324

Conclusion   325

INTRODUCTION

Like a lot of teenagers who wore too much black and had an extensive incense collection, I used to fool around with a tarot deck. I can't remember where I picked it up—some bookstore somewhere. It was exciting to look at all of the images, all of the mysterious men and women fighting with swords or juggling coins or drinking from cups.

But after a few aborted attempts to teach myself to read the cards, I gave up. The manual that came with the cards gave inadequate and confusing definitions—"the Empress: wife, mother, companion"—that detracted from what I was seeing. Unsure of what to do with the cards, I put them away, and they were lost in one move or another.

Ten years later, I came back to the tarot during a particularly difficult time in my life. With the help of a skilled reader, I was able to see my circumstances differently. She helped me find the narrative inside all the muddle. In short, she told me a new story about my life and what I was experiencing. A story I could move through; a story in which I could see how all of the other characters and situations were operating.

After that, I was hooked. I began the slow process of studying the meaning of the tarot and understanding its uses. At the time I worked mostly as a book critic, and I was intrigued by the way the cards could be used as a tool for storytelling. Each reading is, essentially, a story. It begins here, at the center. One card represents you and tells you who you are as the protagonist; others say what's happening to you, what did happen to you, what will happen. Other cards show up as people wandering into your story; others create plot and action.

You lay out the cards, and there on the table you have the outline. You have the who, what, where, and when. You then flesh out that skeleton with your own circumstances, you populate it with the people in your life, and, using the intuitive cues provided by the cards' images, you fit your story onto the story in the cards.

It is not necessarily about telling the future. It is about retelling the present.

After noticing the way the cards hook into your intuition and imagination, I realized that they could easily be used to assist in the creative process. When stuck on a piece, I'd pull some cards to find clarity, or I'd use them to figure out how to structure it. When friends struggled with their book or visual art projects, I'd pull out my deck, and we'd take a look. Soon most of my tarot clients were artists, looking for a little guidance on what to work on next or how to overcome a block.

WHAT IS THE TAROT?

The tarot is a deck of cards designed during the Renaissance. There is debate about whether the cards' origins stretch back further, but for our purposes, we'll stick with what we know for sure.

The deck consists of two parts: the Major Arcana and the Minor

Arcana. The Major Arcana is made up of what you can consider archetypes: the Hermit, Death, the High Priestess, and so on. The Minor Arcana cards illustrate circumstances and conflicts—the kinds of things that add action to a story. The Minor Arcana comes in four suits that correspond with the four elements: Cups (water), Wands (fire), Swords (air), and Coins or Pentacles (earth). Each suit has cards numbering one through ten, and then four court cards: Page, Knight, Queen, and King.

The cards depict the whole realm of human experience, from love to death, from joy to sorrow, from loneliness to friendship. Some cards are particularly nasty; others easily cheer a reader up. But either way, you have to take the dark with the light, just like in life.

The interpretations of the cards change as society changes. The Lovers card, of course, does not require a man and a woman to fulfill its meaning. And at one point, I read in an old tarot book that the Three of Wands indicated that a family member was going to die and leave me a chateau in his or her will. But the Three of Wands no longer means "free chateau"; now it means exploration and adventure. You will experience the cards differently than I will, because they are based on your own experiences and your own philosophy and values. Just because we may have different takes on a card doesn't mean that I can't learn from your interpretations, and I hope you can learn something from mine.

HOW DO I USE THIS BOOK?

As a starting point. Each card has its own thorough interpretation and guidance on how it relates specifically to creativity. I've designed a few new ways to organize the cards for reading what are called "spreads" for different creative problems:

- wanting to start writing or painting or working on your medium of choice, but unsure how to begin;
- restarting a project that has become blocked or lost its way;
- figuring how best to present a project to the world; and
- getting out of a rut to try something new and daring.

The book is also meant to be a source of inspiration. Because I believe firmly in looking to our betters to teach us and guide us, I have included anecdotes of creators throughout time to show how others have overcome obstacles, as well as recommendations of paintings to study, books to read, music to listen to, films to watch, etc.

Remember: the Greeks believed our genius was not part of us but was a divine visitation. Our jobs, as artists and writers, was to become the best possible vessel for that genius. Part of that is to be forever learning, improving, expanding, and experimenting.

QUESTIONS

Is it okay for me to buy my own tarot cards? I read somewhere that your first deck is supposed to be a gift.

It is absolutely okay for you to buy your first tarot deck. That is one of those mystical mumbo-jumbo things designed to make beginners feel inadequate and unwelcome. I have a Virgo moon; I have no time for such nonsense.

Is the tarot just about telling the future?

People have always wanted to know their fates. Will I be rich?

Will I be wise? Will I fall in love? And they have used whatever they had around them to try to sneak a glimpse into the future.

I'm always very curious about the different methods used and the way they were developed. I've had my face read in Chinatown, dragged there by a Malaysian friend who swears it's an accurate, ancient practice. I've had my palm read by people in multiple countries. In Greece, I had my coffee grounds read. I sipped my Turkish coffee while chatting with the very nice woman. Then my cup was inverted on its saucer, and the shape the grounds made was interpreted to tell me my future. I had a woman in the American South read my cards, but she used a deck of playing cards rather than the tarot. I've had my tea leaves read in London, and my astrological chart read in New York City.

There are many other ways to tell your fortune. There's numerology, the telling of your fate by the numbers of your birthday or the number of letters in your name. There's bibliomancy, where you open a book to a random page and line, and through that your future is revealed. There's ceromancy, for which you pour melted wax onto a surface and read the shapes it makes. There's an old Irish New Year's custom that requires you to melt metal and then pour it into cold water. The shape it hardens into will tell you how your year will be. Many believe that your dreams can tell you your future, if you sleep with certain items under your pillow or drink or eat the right things before bed. With pyromancy, you gaze into a fire; with tyromancy, you look at the coagulation of cheese. There's divination by the shapes of clouds, the shapes of the facets of gemstones, the entrails of a sacrificed pigeon or rabbit.

Which is to say that the impulses are all the same. As are the methods, although the medium changes from culture to culture and from person to person. We take an image—this shape of the candle wax or that image on the tarot card—and imbue it with meaning. That meaning is personal to us; it draws something out of us. So if we have been feeling lonely lately, wondering if we will ever see an end to our dry spell and if we'll ever fall in love again, we might see a man's silhouette in that wax.

That doesn't make us foolish or delusional. Maybe it gives us hope. Maybe it prepares something in us. We see that a man is on his way this year, and so we dress up a little. We look around and pay closer attention to the men who swing through our lives. Our depression and loneliness, which maybe had been keeping us isolated by making us unwilling to go out and socialize, lessen and we start trying again. Maybe we meet a man that year because of this or maybe we don't, but maybe in the act of trying—of going out and seeing people again—we start to fall back in love with our own lives, and the whole man thing becomes less of a priority.

We give things meaning by paying attention to them, and so moving your attention from one thing to another can absolutely change your future. Exactly who or what is doing the work here— whether fate is choosing the card, or your unconscious, or random chance—doesn't matter as much as the act of seeing, sensing, and paying attention.

How do the individual cards take on specific meanings? If we're supposed to interpret the images and use our intuition to guide us, all on our own, then why does the Ten of Swords have the same meaning from deck to deck?

In every culture, certain symbols take on certain meanings.

And so the mixing of those symbols, adding an element to a number, to a Greek god, to an astrological marker, would create more complex meanings.

Part of that is the way stories are constructed and understood. And if you establish a meaning for one aspect of the card—say, that Sword refers to air, and air refers to thought and communication—then it makes sense that a story would arise rather naturally from a progression.

Swords is an easy way to understand this, because its progression shows that as the numbers go higher, the darkness of the cards increase. One Sword is a helpful thing to have. You can maneuver it, you can use it as a weapon or as a tool, it is easily carried around—just as one idea or one philosophy can be used as a tool to order your thoughts. But with two swords, things get unwieldy. You either have to choose one and discard the other, or both of your hands are full, and you're not so easily mobile anymore. Just like with two ideas, all of a sudden you have a contradiction, or a choice has to be made. The more you add, the harder it is to carry all of these swords, and the more your mind can spin out of control. So that's part of it.

But mostly the meaning comes from centuries of people writing, thinking, and using the tarot, and sharing their experiences. There is no right or wrong way to think about the tarot, but there are going to be shared meanings.

Let's consider the history of the word *consider*. I'm taking this from Russell A. Lockhart's book *Words as Eggs: Psyche in Language and Clinic*, a kind of psychological etymology book. The other major system of divination and intuitive response of our time is astrology. Now, some people draw the line there. They'll say they "believe" in tarot (*believe* is certainly the wrong word, but it's common parlance; *use* is more accurate) but not in astrology, because they consider astrology fortune-telling. And it can be; some people use it that way, just as they use curds of cheese or shapes of clouds to predict the future. But others of us use it simply as a way to draw our attention to certain parts of our lives and expand our understanding of what's happening to us and with us. It's a way of creating meaning.

The *-sider* part of *consider* comes from the word for "star." Like the word *sidereal*, which means "of or with respect to distant stars." Or *siderated*, which means "planet-struck." A *sidus*, then, was someone who paid attention to the stars. And as this person paid attention to the stars, she would begin to notice certain patterns. When a star or a planet was positioned just so, certain things would happen in her life or in the world. And she would note it. And when there was a different combination of stars, the circumstances would change. And she would note it. And so *consider* started its life as *con-sider*, meaning "*with* the stars." Coexisting.

Our sidus would share her knowledge with another sidus, and so on, until a system of meaning and symbolism was built up. And that's how the rather complex system of astrology was born.

I don't believe in God, so . . .

You can be an atheist and use the tarot. You can be a Christian and use the tarot. There is a long history of writing about chance and synchronicity that has nothing to do with the gods meddling in our realm. (I bet that made you uncomfortable, didn't it?) You get out of the tarot what you put in. It is merely a tool that works on an intuitive, rather than logical, level. No gods required.

What if I'm a total beginner to tarot? Or what if I've never written a thing in my life?

I worked very hard to provide something for everyone, no matter his or her level of expertise. That's both for readers' familiarity with the tarot and for how advanced they are in their creative expression.

That said, it's important to remember there is no right or wrong way to interpret a card. I have been studying tarot for a long time, but I am constantly surprised and learning more. This book is not meant to be the last word on the tarot. Consider it one step in the process, or a friend to help you along the way.

How long does it take to learn the tarot?

It all depends on how often you use the cards and for what purposes, and how much you decide to read and study about them. It took me about eight years before I felt comfortable reading for other people for pay, but you might feel like you've mastered the cards in a year or two.

Which tarot cards should I buy? It seems like there are so many different decks to choose from.

Whichever deck is most comfortable for you is the right tarot deck. There are a lot of options out there. I have several different decks—including the Spolia deck I made with the artist Jen May—and I switch them out, depending on mood. Tarot decks can get a little addictive; the art is so beautiful, and each one has a different feel. My own favorites are the Golden, a contemporary deck that features medieval art; the Haindl, a very complex and nontraditional German deck; and the Minchiate, a Renaissance-era deck that has 96 cards instead of the more standard 78. Each one has its strengths and weaknesses. I find the Minchiate most helpful for creative issues, but I'll almost always turn to the Golden if I have a problem with love. Feel free to experiment. There are online resources such as Facade (www.facade.com) that feature databases of images from a wide range of decks.

Can I read my own cards?

For things like relationship troubles, or money troubles, or Why-do-I-want-to-stab-my-coworker-with-a-screwdriver-every-time-I-see-him? kind of work-related problems, it helps to get an outside perspective. But for daily card draws, for creativity questions, things of that nature, it's pretty easy to read for yourself. If you're still confused, you can always talk to a friend about the cards you drew or swap readings with each other. Don't feel like you always have to fork out money for a professional every time you have a problem.

A FEW THOUGHTS

There is no right or wrong way to express your creativity. There is no perfect way to write a novel, there is no ideal way for a painter to work or for a chef to create a new dish or for a musician to put together a new album. And that is the wonderful and terrifying thing about it. With no rules, how does one keep from getting lost?

I talk to creators all the time who feel like they are wandering around in the dark. They want to know, Why is this taking so long? Why doesn't it work for me the way it seems to work for everyone else? I feel like I'm not making any progress; should I give up?

INTRODUCTION

Nothing kills creativity faster than anxiety: worrying if you're doing things "right," worrying that no one else is going to like what you're doing, panicking about how it's all going to turn out.

Almost every time, the solution is listening to and honoring your intuitive sense of not what you think *you need* but what your *project needs* to come to fruition. Maybe that is the greatest thing the cards can do for us: quiet down our worried thoughts and our expectations for how it's "supposed" to go and help us get back in touch with our imagination.

A HISTORY OF THE TAROT

The history of the deck we recognize as the tarot—the deck that includes both the Minor Arcana and the twenty-two characters and archetypes of the Major Arcana—begins in fifteenth-century Italy. But the tarot came in many different varieties, even from the very beginning. There was a Florentine deck called the Minchiate, with its forty-card Major Arcana set; and a deck from Milan called the Trionfi that used four types of birds rather than the four elements of the standard deck.

Many parts of its origins remain frustratingly obscure. For example, what does the name *tarot* mean? No one really knows, although there are many theories. It comes from the Italian word *tarocco*, which is the name of the card game that the deck was originally used to play. But the word seems to have no other meaning associated with it. (There is a type of blood orange called the *tarocco*, but it's unlikely that the deck was developed as a way of thinking about citrus.) The tarocco cards were simply another version of playing cards, which were designed and played with all over the world, dating back to ninth-century China. They spread from there to Egypt, Persia, Turkey, and beyond. Each culture adapted the cards to create decks of their own and designed different games to match.

1

You might have noticed how closely the Minor Arcana resembles our own standard deck of playing cards with its Aces, the numbers up to ten, and then the royalty cards. The Knight becomes the Jack, the Page is discarded, the Queen and King remain the same. Even the suits match up: hearts to Cups and so on.

Each deck shares a similar origin. So why is one deck used for these mysterious, sometimes occult purposes, while the other is used for play?

The game the cards were designed for, the *tarocco*, has been lost to time. You don't see people playing it anymore. But even as people lost interest in the game, the deck remained. As the tarot cards spread and were adapted by different cities and different cultures, new variations appeared. We still have many examples of these early decks, and many of the distinctive choices of imagery were developed in the fifteenth century and are still found in contemporary decks. The distinctive shape of the Hanged Man's legs—forming a *4*, with one straight leg and one bent knee—can be found in the fifteenth-century Visconti-Sforza deck. The pierced heart of the Three of Swords can also be found in the sixteenth-century Sola Busca deck, originating probably in Venice.

The Sola Busca is one of the few tarot decks that created distinctive imagery for the Minor Arcana. In early versions, most designed these cards the simple way we design playing cards. The Four of Coins has only four coins on it, not the little man clutching his coins to his chest. Many decks added whimsical flourishes, but they weren't necessarily connected to what we understand as being the meaning of the card today. For instance, the monkey gazing at his reflection in a hand mirror on the Minchiate's Four of Cups has long been one of my favorite such flourishes, but I can't say that it's really enhanced my understanding of that particular card.

From Italy, the tarot traveled to France, where the Marseilles deck was developed. This is the template from which most modern decks are derived. The Major Arcana stabilized at this point, settling into the set of twenty-two trumps we use now. Before this, some decks had a Western Emperor and an Eastern Emperor instead of an Empress and an Emperor. But the Marseilles became the template, and the wild variations in the decks faded away and the standard structure emerged.

The Marseilles is also when the tarot began to take on a more, let's say, mystical quality. Alchemical and astrological imagery began to show up on the cards, and it's around this time we have the first evidence that the cards were used for divination as well as game playing. Robert M. Place, in his book *The Tarot: History, Symbolism, and Divination*, points to a cycle of Venetian sonnets called the *Merlini Cocai Sonnets* (Cocai being the pseudonym of the sixteenth-century Italian poet Teofilo Folengo) as containing the first written record of the cards being used for fortune-telling. In the sonnets, the Major Arcana cards are used in a spread to foresee what will happen to the characters of the story.

The written record about the occult use of the tarot begins in about the early eighteenth century. I know what you're thinking (or maybe not; maybe you are less of a history dork than I am): "Hey, isn't that around the time of the Enlightenment? Wasn't the whole point of the Enlightenment to totally get rid of all superstition and irrational belief?"

Yes, that was the point. But here's a little secret: man cannot live on rationality alone. We're not machines; our brains are not computers. You can try to shut off your dream world, your irrationality, your religious beliefs, your need for mystery and greater meaning, and so on, but most of us really do need that side of ourselves. If it were possible for man to be 100 percent rational about all things, then the French writer Voltaire, king of the Enlightenment, probably would not have been a crazy, racist anti-Semite.

So at the time of the Enlightenment there was the Counter-Enlightenment, focused mostly in Germany. The Counter-Enlightenment thinkers argued for more enchantment, more untamed nature, less rationality. You might know these guys as the Romantics. They were philosophers, writers, poets, and artists, although not all of them were German. But they fought against the influence of the Enlightenment and became influential themselves. Which only goes to show that when you stake out a radical position—like, the rational brain is the only thing that matters; all else is a weakness that must be overcome—you are nurturing the extreme opposite of your position into existence as well. (Something that the tarot's Chariot card knows very well.)

Part of the Counter-Enlightenment was the development of mystery cults. Starting in the seventeenth century, we had Freemasonry and Rosicrucianism. Both developed and spread esoteric knowledge, although you had to be an initiated member to learn their secrets. Moving on, we had theosophy and Swedenborgianism, which were radically new religions, heavy on the mystical and philosophical side of belief. In the nineteenth century, the Counter-Enlightenment spread to America with Spiritualism, and then names you're probably more familiar with: groups like the Hermetic Order of the Golden Dawn, people like Madame

Blavatsky (aka Helena Petrovna Blavatsky, the Russian occultist who cofounded the Theosophical Society), and so on. The Golden Dawn and other groups like it believed in magic, and in the ability of the human will to change matter and the course of events.

The question of why all of these systems started to develop around the same time is an interesting one. It was obviously answering a need in people; otherwise it wouldn't have spread the way it did. Part of that has to do with the Enlightenment and this focus on the rational mind, but part of that also can be traced to the evolution that Christianity was going through.

Christianity was the dominant religion of the West. Protestantism was relatively new, but it had taken a firm hold. And the Catholic Church adapted to survive against the Protestant ideas, lest its power wane. Christianity was becoming more of a moral code—a system of preferred behaviors and a way of controlling the populace—than before. Church services had been a sensory experience, with incense and religious art and music and chanting, all designed to move a person spiritually and to create altered states, if you will. But the Protestant iconoclasts, who believed that religious imagery was idolatry, had destroyed much of the religious art and emptied the churches of their adornments. In place of the music and chanting came lectures on morality: don't do this; do this instead.

I am oversimplifying this to preserve space, but there is an enormous difference in the role of religion in the medieval church and its subsequent role post-Reformation. Some of the primary differences were the removal of artwork and imagery from the religious ceremonies, increased policing of behavior, and de-emphasizing the role of mystery and intuition in a person's life.

But by staking out their radical position, they nurtured their extreme opposite's position, too. That sense of magic and wonder had answered a call in the human soul, and so it could not be discarded so quickly. New systems of belief, which put the mystery at the very heart of its teachings, began to develop. The cults themselves might have disappeared by now, but much of what they revived interest in, from tarot to astrology to meditation, can be found in contemporary culture with the rise of Wicca and other pagan religions and other systems of (I mean this affectionately) irrational belief.

The Golden Dawn had probably the most influence on our contemporary understanding of the tarot. For this group of magicians and mystics, it was one tool of many in their magical system that pulled from sources like the Rosicrucians and the Kabbalah. One of the Golden Dawn's founders, Samuel Liddell MacGregor Mathers, wrote the first guide to the tarot in England. *The Tarot: Its Occult Signification, Use in Fortune-Telling and Methods of Play*, published in 1888, the same year the Golden Dawn came into existence, established tarot as a magical tool, and standardized the deck (or tried to—variations soon emerged) into the four suits of Wands, Cups, Swords, and Pentacles.

The Golden Dawn actually didn't last very long. Infighting and power plays, mostly by the male members, splintered the group. Its most famous member was perhaps the Irish poet William Butler Yeats, who remained interested in and engaged with magical systems until his death. The writer and magician Aleister Crowley is often associated with the group, but he was quickly ejected from its ranks for being a terrible person. (This is a fact, he was a terrible person. Look it up.) But two of its lesser-known members would spread the influence of the tarot far and wide: writer Arthur Edward Waite and artist Pamela Colman Smith.

While Mathers might have standardized the deck's layout, Waite and Smith standardized its imagery. Their deck is typically called the Rider-Waite, but it should be called the Rider-Waite-Smith because Smith was at the very least an equal partner in its creation. Almost every deck on the market today follows its templates of imagery and meaning. The major exception is the Thoth tarot, designed by Crowley and Lady Frieda Harris and taking its name from the Egyptian god of knowledge, which uses the Princess instead of the Page and switches the placement of Strength and Justice, along with some other noticeable changes. But by far, the Thoth deck has not had the reach of the Rider-Waite-Smith.

So how did the deck come about? A. E. Waite was a mystic and a scholar with ties to both the Golden Dawn and the Freemasons. He had written extensively on many esoteric subjects, such as alchemy, mysticism, and the various mystery cults to which he belonged. Here Waite's scholarly and mystical interests played an important role in the fate of the tarot.

Waite believed that the magical systems of the Golden Dawn and other systems were not about imposing your will on a situation (making someone love you, increasing your wealth, and so on) or about telling the future (Will this person love you? Will you ever be wealthy?). He believed they were for elevating the soul and for bringing what is unconscious conscious. He believed there was a divine order, and our job was to align ourselves with it or become a conduit, like the Magician in the tarot.

It's like the difference between a $5 palm reader and a spiritual adviser. The palm reader is, in a sense, going to tell you what you want to hear. Or tell you that the reason you are single is that you are cursed, and you need to buy this $35 candle and this $10 prayer guide to help rid yourself of the curse or you will die alone. That type of reading preys on people's hopes and fears. The spiritual adviser, instead, will focus on why you compulsively do the same thing over and over again, and will bring to light your darkest fears—not to take advantage of them but to help you see what they really are. It's about elevating you as a person and as a soul.

For Waite, there is a higher purpose for a person's existence, and mysticism is a tool to find that purpose and follow it. To help that process along best, he would need a tarot deck that was designed with these goals specifically in mind. The deck, he thought, needed to be reworked with an emphasis on its symbolism and symbolism's connection to the intuition. First, he needed an artist.

Smith was brought to the Golden Dawn by her friend Yeats. A talented artist, she had illustrated books by both Yeats and Bram Stoker (best remembered for the vampire tale *Dracula*) by the time she was introduced to Waite. He was struck by her use of symbolism and by her artistry, and they began their collaboration.

For a long time, it was assumed that Smith simply drew what Waite told her to draw. That she was, in a way, just taking his dictation. But recent scholarship suggests that she was much more in control of the imagery and the symbolism than thought previously. Waite provided much of the scholarship, and in many cases the imagery of the Sola Busca provided inspiration, but Smith brought her own talent and knowledge to the deck, and it's a shame that she has been sidelined from the story for so long. (Incidentally, the "Rider" part of the name comes from the original publisher of the deck, William Rider & Sons. So the British publisher gets credit, but not the artist.)

The Rider-Waite-Smith differed from most decks in one important aspect: for the first time since the Sola Busca, all of the cards, including the Minor Arcana, were fully illustrated with human figures and other symbolic imagery. This is the full separation mark of the tarot from a deck of playing cards to a deck of divination cards. And this is where much of the meaning of the Minor Arcana cards became consolidated. Most of that is due to Smith's artwork. Waite wrote a few guides to the tarot, manuals on how to interpret each card, but Smith's imagery is what people remember, not Waite's definitions. Waite believed it was his writings and scholarship that would newly define the tarot, but it turns out that sometimes the brush is even more powerful than the pen.

Which brings us to today. There have been many successful tarot decks since the Rider-Waite-Smith, like the Aquarius deck and the Morgan-Greer, both developed in the 1970s when the New Age movement started to gain mainstream acceptability, but almost all have followed the illustrative choices that Smith made. It's all but impossible to overstate her importance in how we use and think about the tarot today.

We don't know the full history of tarot, but these are the elements that helped create it. Humans searching for meaning discover it in the everyday things they have lying around. They pay attention to and consider the patterns of the cards. They share their knowledge with others, who then expand on those meanings. They tell one another stories about the cards, thereby creating even more complex patterns and meanings. And then it becomes as if we were never without them.

A HISTORY OF ARTISTS AND TAROT

Ever since those sixteenth-century Venetian sonnets mentioned before, artists and writers have been drawn to the tarot, have written about it and pulled from the imagery for their own work. Some were so taken with the experience of reading tarot that they dedicated themselves to constructing entirely new decks.

It's easy to see why artists in particular connect to the deck. Tarot readers tell stories—stories that might not always have a logical sense but have instead an intuitive meaning. The story is guided by a feeling, or perhaps the mood a color suggests to the reader, or strange coincidences in the pictures. (For instance, on one card, three figures are hunched over their work, so that might be relevant because . . .) That is a creative act. And so artists, used to working in that way, often take to the decks like ducks to water.

We'll focus our attention here on the twentieth-century post–Golden Dawn, around the time that Waite and Smith were redefining the tarot for a new age.

The obvious place to begin is with the surrealists. The surrealists wanted to engage directly with the unconscious in their artwork; to put aside reason and logic—they deemed reason and logic to be tyrannical—and work with dream imagery and illogical narratives to express something different and powerful.

The surrealists came out of the Dada movement, which had decided to respond to the nonsensical violence, warmongering, dehumanization, and industrialization of the age with a purer form of nonsense. Led by the Romanian-born writer Tristan Tzara, Dada performances were mostly jangling noise. One person yelling strange words as atonal music blurted and blasted and women in bizarre costumes danced around the stage with seemingly no choreography worked out at all. The Dada artists were simply re-creating what modern life had become: stupid advertising slogans and mottoes, juxtaposed against the noise of urban life, the barking of mad totalitarian leaders, and the never-ending machine of war that slaughtered and maimed an entire generation of men.

Even the Dada manifesto, written by Tzara, makes a wonderful kind of intuitive sense without being what anyone would call "logical":

"Dada is a dog—a compass—the lining of the stomach—neither new or a nude Japanese girl—a gasometer of jangled feelings—Dada is brutal and doesn't go in for propaganda—Dada is a quantity of life in transparent, effortless and gyratory transformation."

Every time the manifesto accidentally veers toward being logical, it swerves hard away again. It cannot be "understood," but it can be enjoyed. Once one stops fighting against the absurdity and embraces it, one can see it in a different context.

Surrealism was a response to Dada. Instead of being so far on the edges of insanity, they wanted to give voice to the unconscious. They wanted to create artistic versions of the dream world, which they believed was not just random and bizarre but, instead, worked according to its own sense of logic and truth. Their artwork relied heavily on the idea of the symbol: an image that might look simple but has a deep impact on the viewer; something that represents a big idea and calls to something beneath the surface.

Which is, essentially, what the imagery of the tarot does as well. Every gesture, every color, every archetype and figure stands in for something greater, something very personal and meaningful to us. It's no wonder, then, that surrealists were drawn to the tarot.

This was obviously very much inspired by the work of the Austrian neurologist Sigmund Freud, father of psychoanalysis. The discovery of the unconscious was tremendous and had a huge impact on the way people saw themselves. Suddenly we realized that we don't have complete control over our actions, that we are driven by desires and impulses we have no way of understanding logically. Deviance and mental illness were no longer caused by failures of self-discipline, or a willful inability to keep it together. There are things happening in our brains and in our lives that we cannot affect with reason, nor can they be brought to light with logic.

But maybe art could be the bridge between these two states; the light of reason and the darkness of the unconscious. The unconscious, after all, does not speak in verbal language. It speaks in the language of dreams, symbols, and ritual. It could be reached only by using its own methods. That is what the surrealists were trying to do. Creators such as Leonor Fini, Claude Cahun, the British-born painter Leonora Carrington and her onetime lover German artist Max Ernst used archetypes and symbolism and the uncanny and dream imagery to create unreal states; art that could be understood better on an emotional level than on an intellectual level.

Their tools were automatic writing—the writer would write down whatever came to mind, no matter how silly or strange, trying not to control or judge the writing or where it would go—and psychoanalysis, dream imagery, and things like the tarot. Salvador Dalí, arguably the most famous surrealist artist, was particularly intrigued by the tarot, and he seems to have been introduced to the cards by his wife, Gala. She was the more esoteric of the two, and her interest in the occult is well documented.

Late in his life, Dalí decided to create his own deck of tarot cards. He worked from the basic definitions of the cards as outlined by Waite and Smith, but he deviated from their basic templates. He used images that came to him in dreams, alongside ancient Roman and Christian iconography to create a very surrealist deck. Where Smith created clean, simple to understand images, Dalí designed bizarre landscapes. The great Spanish artist was nearing the end of his life, and his cards' images are based on a lifetime of knowledge of art history, the power of the icon and the symbol, and many figures—such as his strangely elegant elephants with long, spidery legs—that recurred in his artwork throughout his career.

It's not just visual artists who were drawn to the tarot. Writers have used the cards as a storytelling technique for centuries now. That ranges from the hokey (a young adult protagonist visits a fortune-teller who reveals her true fate via the cards, which sends her off on a grand adventure, and so on) to the more sophisticated.

Many writers have turned to the occult and the mysterious to assist them with their writing. There were many writers in the Golden Dawn, although Yeats was probably the most vocal about his use of magic in his writing process. As well as being one of the greatest writers of the twentieth century, he was also a pretty adept magician. The archetypes from the Major Arcana show up in many of his poems, but he also used them for divination and self-reflection.

Yeats used many occult systems in his writing. He was married to Bertha Georgie Hyde-Lees, a skilled medium who was also a member of the Golden Dawn. Together they used Ouija boards and automatic writing to contact the spirit realm, but also more classic systems such as astrology and tarot. This renewed interest in the occult reinvigorated his dedication to poetry, and led to some of his greatest work. Much of Yeats's late-career poems drew directly on the revelations he received through séances and divination rituals. He stated that the spirit realm gave him the metaphors he used in his poetry, and many of those metaphors—"Slouches towards Bethlehem" and "the centre cannot hold," both from his 1919 poem "The Second Coming"—have become common phrases in our culture.

Other writers, though, were more interested in the tarot as a narrative tool. Because a tarot spread like the Celtic Cross is essentially a method of storytelling, writers have latched onto the cards as a way of structuring work.

Let's look for a minute at the Celtic Cross. It is the standard tarot spread; probably the one most in use around the world. The cards are arranged in two forms: a cross to the left, and a tower to the right. The cards in the cross illuminate a person's motivations, what she is thinking and feeling, where she has been, and where she is going. The tower names the character with a card that represents the querent—the fancy tarot term for the person asking the question—directly and provides an ending to the story with the final outcome card.

The Celtic Cross reading is powerful because it contains all of the elements needed to tell a basic story. It has a beginning, a middle, and an end for the plot. It gives us characters and tells us what those characters want. There is a conflict, there is a goal. There are subplots, and a person's deepest fears are revealed. One could conceivably lay out a Celtic Cross reading and use it to construct an entire novel.

The Celtic Cross Spread

Which is exactly what the Italian writer Italo Calvino did. He was not a specialist in the cards. He stated on more than one occasion that his interest in tarot was not scholarly, nor was he interested in learning how to read the cards skillfully. He found the people on the cards fascinating, as well as all the different interpretations—all the ways a story could be told simply by the patterns that one could create by laying out the cards randomly.

Calvino's interest in the tarot resulted in the 1973 novel *The Castle of Crossed Destinies*. There a group of travelers have been mysteriously robbed of voice. But they are able to reconstruct the story of what happened to them using the images on the tarot cards.

Calvino was long interested in fables, fairy tales, mythology, and other archetypal writings, and so he was accustomed to exploring the power that story has over the unconscious. And despite not having a deep knowledge of the cards' meanings, Calvino understood how a person creates meaning out of whatever is around them, and how story is one of the most powerful tools for creating a meaningful narrative out of the chaos and random occurrences that make up our lives.

This is where Calvino meets up with the Swiss psychologist Carl Jung and his followers. Both understood fairy tales' layered levels of meaning. There is the surface story of a girl in a tower, or a witch in the forest, or a knight sent off on a quest. Then there is the way the story becomes an archetypal tale that we can relate directly back to our own lives. "Rapunzel" is not the story of a girl trapped in a tower; it is the story of how after we've experienced a trauma, we can wall ourselves up to avoid getting hurt again but, in doing so, inadvertently prevent ourselves from falling in love or experiencing life as well. "Little Red Riding Hood" is not the story of a girl trying to visit her grandmother; it's the story of the dark and sometimes terrifying encounter with one's own sexuality.

Of course, when you're reading these stories as a child, you're not aware of any of this. And yet these stories have a strong grip on our imagination, and the imagery stays with us. The girl dressed in red, wandering in the dark and pursued by an unseen threat—how many times have we seen that image reworked and restaged in works of art? Many historians and therapists, like the great British writer Marina Warner, believe that one purpose of the fairy tale is to impart knowledge to children about how to live in a dangerous world. Sometimes your stepmother really does want to kill you; sometimes predators (both the human and the animal kinds) really do want to devour you.

The images of the tarot hew closely to images from fairy tales, from the kings and queens and knights to Rapunzel's tower. The Five of Coins could be retold as "The Little Match Girl," the King of Coins could be related as the story of King Midas, and so on.

Calvino, both in *Castle* and his other writings, worked extensively with fairy-tale story lines and imagery. Travelers lost in snowstorms and forests, magical and inexplicable happenings, characters of royalty, peasantry, and nomads. There's a man who climbs into a tree and refuses to come down. There are cities built out of words, cities built out of dreams. So, of course, a writer like that would be drawn to the tarot—they all spring from the same realm.

But there is another aspect to the tarot and similar systems that we have not discussed yet, and that is the randomness of the draw. You have a deck of cards, ranging in number from seventy-eight to over a hundred, depending on the design, and from that you draw a set number of cards at random. Coincidence rules which cards come out and in what order.

Now, coincidence can be seen as being meaningful or not. Certainly Carl Jung—who was a great fan of the tarot and astrology—would see coincidence as meaningful. It is our unconscious guiding our hands; it is an outer reflection of our inner state. He called it synchronicity, or "meaningful coincidence." Synchronicity can be explained a bit like this: You know how sometimes you are thinking all day long of someone you haven't heard from in years, and then that person emails or calls you? That is a meaningful coincidence. It wasn't the power of our thoughts that caused him or her to call us; the coincidence is that both you and this person were moved simultaneously to think of the other, like some impulse springing up from the memory banks.

Synchronous events become meaningful in part because of our

inability to explain them away. The coincidence can stun you and make you look for a larger reason as to why it occurred. I'll give you an example from my own life.

I had been complaining to a mentor of mine about being overlooked at work. I did all of the grunt work but was not getting any of the credit. I felt like I was seen as being unremarkable—that no one could see, let alone would reward, my talents—and I worried about always being stuck doing the boring, menial tasks. My mentor listened. Then she told me a fairy tale about a little wren who sweeps up after everyone has left the party, but whom no one ever notices. Eventually the little wren becomes the king by being crafty and smart and by paying attention to everything around her. Her invisibility becomes useful.

A few weeks after this conversation, I was working in my home office when I heard furious chirping and a crash. I looked over, and my (indoor) cat had somehow caught a wren that had flown in through an open window; she was sitting there with it flapping away in her mouth. I pried the little bird out of my cat's mouth—it was in shock but mostly okay. I locked my cat away in a room while she howled in furious protest, and I climbed onto my fire escape with the wren in my hands. We stayed there for an hour, me holding the tiny frightened bird until she felt okay enough to fly away. I went back into my apartment and checked the mail. In it was a letter from my mentor, with a printout of the wren fairy tale she had mentioned over the phone.

To me, that day has a powerful significance. I can't quite figure out how the wren got into the apartment or why, I can't figure out how my lazy cat who is terrified of the open windows managed to catch it, and I can't figure out why or how this coincided with the arrival of the letter. And yet it is all the more meaningful because of this. Or, perhaps, if any of this were to be understood logically and the coincidence explained easily, it would drain the day of meaning. Instead, that story of the wren has guided me through all sorts of difficult situations and setbacks, and the wren has become a powerful talisman.

In the Jungian way, then, our tarot spreads are not random but are guided by the same principle. A particular card will show up because, in some way, we need it to. We are not causing the cards to fall the way they do, but each card is a meaningful coincidence. The fact that we can't explain why we get the Five of Wands when we're going through a very Five of Wands situation—a manuscript that comes back with yet another round of extensive edits, or a teacher who frustrates you by pointing out what you're doing wrong instead of congratulating you on the improvements you've made—makes it more meaningful. During a reading I once gave, I decided to use the Golden tarot, despite it not being my usual go-to deck. My client drew the Page of Wands to represent her own self and noticed that the scroll depicted on the card was the exact shape of the tumor they had just found on her kidney. That small coincidence gave the reading a special meaning for her.

Then there are those who respond not to the synchronicity but to the randomness itself. The meaning*less* part of it. The twentieth-century avant-garde composer John Cage provides perhaps the best example/way to explain this part of it, even though he chose the I Ching over the tarot to help him compose his projects, the most famous of these being his *Music of Changes*. The ancient Chinese text, said to date as far back as the tenth century BC, is similar to the tarot, except that it uses tiles or coins rather than tarot cards, and a large book that helps you interpret the patterns formed when you conduct a reading. Cage would ask a question about the composition he was working on, cast the tiles, and then use the answers found in the book to make changes to the music.

Cage was not the only artist to rely on the I Ching to make structural decisions about his work. The prolific author Philip K. Dick relied on the divination system while writing *The Man in the High Castle* (1962), his speculative historical novel about a world in which the Nazis and Imperial Japan won World War II.

But for Cage, it was the randomness of the I Ching that interested him. He wanted to break conventional structures, he wanted to spotlight not what he could control by writing but what he could not control—such as his compositions of silence, where the music becomes the unintentional sounds of the audience: coughing, shuffling feet, the sounds of people flipping the pages of their concert program. So his interest was in refusing to make decisions and losing authorial control over what is happening. The notes, tempo, and just about every other element were decided upon by casting the coins and not by any overarching vision on his part.

As you can see, there is much to draw on from the tarot in the artistic process. What interests you in the cards will be something unique: something about you and your interests, or maybe something I miss entirely in this book. But there's no right way and no wrong way to use the cards. There are all sorts of different points of inspiration that come from the deck.

MY OWN HISTORY WITH THE TAROT

My first real engagement with the tarot came when I was in my late twenties. Like many people who take up the cards, I was inspired by a really good reading.

I'd had readings before, but none of them were that interesting. A few done by friends after I left high school—the deck was usually pulled out after a couple glasses of wine, and, of course, there was only good news to share. Love and happiness, coming right up! The fact that love and happiness never seemed to show up on schedule seemed a little suspicious. Then there were the cranks: the storefront card readers sitting in shops cloudy with incense and a few giant crystals scattered about. They told me mostly that I had a dark cloud hovering over me and if I bought this sacred candle and paid for them to pray for me, we could dispel it together.

My interest in the cards remained, even through disastrous readings. I had bought a deck of my own, but I never really got past the phase of needing to look up the meaning of every card in the manual, which meant that the readings were not really telling me much. "Am I the Queen, or is that someone else? And if so, who?" "The manual says the Five of Coins means financial hardship, but I'm actually doing okay with money right now; I don't get it." The cards had potential, I thought. I just couldn't tap into it.

Then there was a difficult time. Financially, ambitiously, professionally, romantically, socially. You know those times in your life when you realize that every single thing you had going for you had decided to flee at the same time? It was that. In a fit of exasperation, a friend—one who'd had to drag me out of bars by my hair to keep me away from terrible men, grab glasses of whiskey out of my hand, and hand me tissues when I started crying in public yet again—booked me a session with her own tarot reader. "You need to get it together" I think was how she framed it.

After years of gentle readings by well-intentioned friends who wanted to see only joy in my future, I expected more of the same.

And sure, there is a buzz that follows someone telling you that everything is going to be all right, and maybe that would last long enough that I could at least wash my hair again or put on pants every day for a week. I was ready to hand over some money and suspend disbelief in exchange for just enough optimism to get me out of my apartment on a regular basis, even if that optimism would prove fleeting.

But when I showed up at my tarot card reader's apartment, I was surprised. And, dare I say, a little disappointed? I was ready for the witch stuff: the incense and the crystals and the long beads. Instead, I found a woman with a Bronx accent and a tasteful apartment. She was wearing tailored black pants and shirt and leopard-print kitten heels. I envied her bookshelves full of beautiful art books. I was only a little bit in love with her already.

The tarot reader continued to defy my expectations. She didn't read the cards by the book. Nor did she sugarcoat anything. She pointed to the Knights—dignified warriors when they are fighting valiantly, but bringers of chaos when they are not directed intelligently—who seemed to be waging war against minor characters. The Tower was there, sure, but it was contained safely in the "Hopes and Fears" position of the Celtic Cross spread, not actually in play. "It's like you're drowning in a birdbath," she told me. "Stand up, it's just a birdbath."

I almost wanted to pout. You mean, I was going to have to actually take responsibility for what was going on in my life? Admit that I was responding to changing circumstances by walking into the middle of the street, rending my garments, and yelling, "Help, I am dying!" when I was actually pretty fine? Who wants that?

But the reading settled on me. And eventually I realized that maybe my coping strategy of booze, men, and weeping warranted plotting a new course.

Mostly what I wanted to do was to learn how to read the cards, or at least read them like she had. She had done something clever. She had taken what I had thought was happening in my life and told me a different story. I wasn't dying, nor was my life such a disaster. I was responding poorly to the disappointment of my life not going exactly the way I wanted and was, frankly, being a bit of a baby about it. She had pointed out where I could make changes; how I could redirect those Knights and use them for good. It was thrilling to watch her work, to see her construct the story and hand out wisdom casually, all in an hour-long session.

So began the long learning process. I should warn you: learning from a book will take you only so far. A book, like the one you are reading now, can teach you good, basic definitions of the cards. But for a broader view of the cards, you're going to have to get your hands dirty.

There's no program that will make you a master of the cards in thirty days or less, I found. Once I had the cards' meanings memorized—in that I didn't have to keep looking back at the manual to remind myself what each card represented—the real training began.

I started by drawing one card a day and just seeing what happened during that day. I looked for the situation on the card to show itself in my life. (I write more about this process, and how you can replicate it, in the "How to Do a Reading" chapter.) I would pull the Seven of Wands and then notice how I felt like I was bashing heads against everyone I came in contact with—including my own not-so-helpful thoughts and anxiety. I would pull the Ten of

Swords and notice all of the ways I was trying to sustain friendships, relationships, or work projects that were better abandoned.

Noticing—paying attention—is the first step. Making those cards useful to you is the next step. I would pull the Nine of Swords and realize that I really had to figure out the source to my sleepless nights. What exactly was the root of the anxiety that would shake me awake at four in the morning? And what could be done about it? The Nine of Swords made me notice I could do something about this, not just suffer through it. I would pull the Three of Cups and notice how long it had been since I invited my female friends over for a dinner party, and then send out emails instantly.

Then there was a long process of giving messy readings to my friends. Getting it wrong, backtracking, blushing furiously as I said, "Actually, that's not right, let me think," and then staring at the cards in silence for a long time while I tried to figure things out. Bless them, they stuck with me. It gradually became easier and easier to understand how the cards worked together, as well as how to construct the story, how not to rely on just the rigid textbook definitions of the cards and find something more expansive and intuitive.

During this time, the questions I had for myself had mostly to do with my work, which is writing. (Also the usual number of frantic heartbroken crazy readings, but that is par for the course.) I found the Celtic Cross unhelpful as a way of investigating my problems with the writing process, and I found that when I asked other people for readings, their lack of experience in the area stunted the potential scope of the reading. My tarot card reader is wonderful, but going to her for a writing problem felt a bit like going to a general practitioner for glaucoma treatment. Sometimes you need a specialist.

I've long been fascinated by the creative process and by stories of artistic people I admired: how they worked, how they thought, how they found inspiration. I read biography after biography and absorbed everything they had to offer. I read about how Coco Chanel designed her first major hit—a little straw boater hat—simply because the heavy nineteenth-century hats piled with feathers and fabric and jewels, often weighing several pounds, gave her neck problems. I read about how Margaret Anderson started a small literary magazine called the *Little Review*, which ended up publishing all of the truly great writers of the early twentieth century, from James Joyce to Ezra Pound, before they became famous. I read about how the British writer Arthur Koestler was sentenced to death during the Spanish Civil War—which he was covering as a journalist—after being captured by the Nationalists and brought up on charges of supporting the communists, and how that inspired his 1940 masterpiece *Darkness at Noon*.

And then I started to see how these artists related to the tarot. Coco Chanel became the Queen of Wands, the woman who builds an empire out of her own desires. Margaret Anderson's magazine came to represent the Ten of Coins to me, the little village that shares the bounty, that inspires one another and works together. Koestler came to represent the Strength card, able to withstand the most devastating of circumstances and keep his head, wait things out until the situation improves (he was released from prison), and still create something beautiful out of it.

I started to develop my own readings, built specifically to help me with my own process. And they helped—tremendously. So much so that I started to think I should start offering my own services as a reader. By this time, I had been studying the tarot for eight years. I felt confident that I did a good job at it. I felt like I had a unique perspective to provide.

Over the years, I've read cards for young-adult novelists, photographers, poets, singers, painters, and dancers. I've talked to some about feeling blocked and like they might never create anything new again, and I've listened to others talk about their need to make space within their marriage or family for time to work. We've covered projects that seem to have lost their way, disappointments with how their work was received, and their feeling that they were barely making progress. I've learned so much from these conversations, and I hope I've contributed enough to them, too.

Becoming a tarot reader was never my plan. I was more than a little surprised at how quickly it took over my life. How fascinating I found the cards, and how eagerly I dug into their history, how I couldn't get enough of reading about the Golden Dawn, psychology, and art and music. Or how much I enjoyed the conversations I had with my clients and how my sessions felt more like play than work.

Designing my own deck, the Spolia tarot, with my amazing collaborator Jen May, a collage artist from Brooklyn, has given me a whole new understanding of the cards. You will find illustrations from our deck here in this book. The history and meaning of each card was researched extensively before it was designed, and I'm very proud of the result.

This book is, then, just the first step. Like every new skill you pick up, you'll get better at it the more you do it and the better you understand it. Let it be fun.

And with that, let's start introducing you to the cards themselves.

THE CARDS

The first step is familiarizing ourselves with the cards.

MAJOR ARCANA

The deck begins with the Major Arcana, twenty-two trumps representing archetypal figures and situations. The cards tell a story in themselves, beginning with our naive little Fool, traveling on his journey, gaining certain skills, facing calamity and healing, mastery and self-destruction, until the Fool achieves wholeness with the World.

The cards in the Major Arcana are more archetypal, or allegorical, than the rest of the deck. Their meanings are more complex and often have to be understood through their own stories. These are the big moments of our lives: love, birth, death, change. When you pull a Major Arcana, there is rarely any doubt what it refers to; it is often where your life has been the most dramatic lately.

MINOR ARCANA

Then we move on to the Minor Arcana. These numbered cards concern situations that we encounter in our daily lives and the choices we have to make. While the Major Arcana might feel like things that happen *to us*, the Minor Arcana feel like the things that *we do* in the world.

Things separate out there by suit, going from the Ace to the King in the suits of Swords, Cups, Wands, and Coins.

SWORDS

These represent air and the intellectual function: thought, communication, logic, and reason. The Swords align naturally with writing simply because the suit rules the acts of communication and thinking. If it helps you to visualize the cards' meaning, you could envision a human body, and align the Swords card with the head and all of its functions: seeing, hearing, reading, thinking, and talking.

CUPS

The Cups represent water, and so they rule the emotional realm, from love to hate and back again—but also intuition and any kind of spiritual feeling. Anything that moves us, particularly film and visual art, falls under Cups. On our chart of the body, the Cups would reside in the heart.

WANDS

The Wands (which might be called the suit of Rods or Staffs in some decks) represent fire. Their mode is to be the desiring, passionate, creative force. Performance, which should light both the performer and the audience on fire, is ruled by Wands. But this suit is also required to spark a new project, build enthusiasm, and give the artist the energy required. Not to be old-fashioned about it, but the Wands would make their home in the loins.

COINS

The Coins (which might be called the suit of Pentacles in some decks) represent the element of earth, or anything that is tangible and made of matter. Artistically, sculpture is a natural Coins medium, but all finished products, if they exist in the world, have to end here. This suit also represents the act of work. On the body, the Coins would be the feet, keeping us grounded and planted on the earth.

COURT CARDS

The court cards—Pages, Knights, Queens, and Kings—are the other people in our lives, but they are also aspects of ourselves. So when you draw a court card, you'll have to do a little self-examination to determine whether this is a characteristic of yourself that you've been displaying lately, or whether it is someone you know who is influencing you, for good or bad.

It would be helpful if you read this book alongside a deck of cards. As I said in the introduction, there's no need to be "gifted" your first deck—you don't need to wait for the gods to bestow them upon you—just go out and buy one. Find one that works for you; it does not have to be the Rider-Waite-Smith.

I've divided up the explanations for the cards into a few different sections. First, I describe the imagery of the card, or at least the parts most important for understanding its meaning. I use the Rider-Waite-Smith as my guide here, because it is the most standard. Your own deck might differ.

Then I move into the basic definition of the card. You can use these for any type of reading; it doesn't have to concern creativity. I wanted to give a little background for people who are beginners to the deck. If you are someone who has been using the tarot for a while, these will not be of much use to you, except maybe as a refresher.

Then we come to how the cards relate to artistic projects. I've taken stories from biographies, from my clients, from the worlds of film and literature and music of how artists have dealt with problems in their process. How musicians battled their record companies for the right to record their music their way. Or how a writer overcame losing everything he'd ever written when his wife left their suitcase on a train. Or how a composer dealt with the humiliation of a riot at his opera's premiere.

I lined up these stories with a tarot card that describes a similar situation. Standing up for what you believe in is a Seven of Wands kind of thing, and so I placed it there. Perhaps if you draw the same card during a reading, you can use that person's story as an inspiration for you to find the same strength. Losing a manuscript and needing to start over is the destructive element of the Tower. Dealing with disappointment and humiliation corresponds with the Five of Cups.

These stories should also give wider meaning to the cards, to show how they work in the real world. How people respond to these quandaries can give you ideas on how you might respond to your own. And they help relate the cards more directly to the artistic experience.

And finally, I've included some recommended materials to go along with each card: films, books, songs, poems, paintings, and so on. Some of these recommendations illustrate the card's deeper meaning, like the film *Auntie Mame* for the Nine of Cups. The self-contained happiness and pleasure of that card is shown in the world-traveling, party-throwing, joyful, and wise spinster aunt. Other recommendations are the finished product of the block or obstacle that is outlined in the stories of the cards, like David Bowie's 1972 album *The Rise and Fall of Ziggy Stardust and the Spiders from Mars*, which represents the Star's need for you to be the quirky, eccentric genius that you are, even if people look at you funny. These lists are in no way complete; just consider them little samplers to guide you on your journey.

I've also included the recommended materials because I believe strongly in cross-pollination. I think that writers should be inspired by visual art, filmmakers by music, sculptors by poetry and so on. I also believe that artists should know their artistic history and be knowledgeable about all the art the world has to offer. It not only inspires but also refines your senses and your skills. I push all of my clients to delve into the history of art as much as possible. Not only the art they are naturally drawn to but also—maybe even more importantly—to art that repels them. The goal is to educate them-selves and to understand their own artistic lineage. Remember, a limited budget is not an obstacle to your education when there are libraries to supply these books and films, and online databases are available for visual art. I've listed a lot of individual paintings and artists here, and if they are unfamiliar to you, a simple search online will bring them up.

You'll find that the longer you use the cards and work to chase down their meanings, the more nuanced and substantial they will become for you. The more they seem to encompass, the more in the world you see to relate back to them. You'll be reading a book or watching a film, and the archetypes will start to reveal themselves to you. They are a limitless resource creatively; a well that will never run dry. And paying attention is, of course, the first step in understanding the cards.

And with all of that in mind, let's begin. With the Fool.

·•- THE FOOL - 0 -•·

A figure, carrying very few belongings but seemingly at the beginning of a long journey, walks under blue skies and a burning sun. He or she is about to step off the edge of a cliff, but either does not care or has not yet noticed.

The Fool generally represents faith, in both its bad (naivete) and good (trust and honesty) forms. The Fool steps off the edge of the cliff into nothingness because he or she expects the universe to break the fall. It is represented by the number zero.

The Fool is a fantastic card to draw when you're beginning a new project, because it means you're off on a big adventure. He's the very first card in the deck—he doesn't even begin at one, he starts at zero. And so that is often what the Fool represents: a new beginning, an impassioned start.

If he shows up when we're already in the middle of a project, however, it's his energy that we need to embrace. The Fool walks into the world with no big plan for where he'll end up, and certainly no map. He just starts and trusts that he'll figure it out as he goes along. It's also a card of faith, both in yourself and in the universe or whatever you would like to call that, to deal with any complication or problem that might arise along the way. If you've been feeling particularly down on yourself or on your work, the Fool asks you to embrace optimism instead, to move past your doubts.

It's a bit like the Mr. Magoo card of the deck. Remember that old TV cartoon character? The nearsighted old man who can't see past the nose on his face, and yet he stumbles out into the world anyway. He steps off of buildings, not seeing the drop below, but is caught by a crane at the construction site next door just in time. He walks into traffic, but the cars all manage to swerve around him. He just barely survives his trip to the grocery store, every day.

That's the kind of energy you need to bring into your project. For writers, that would mean plowing through a first draft, without constantly criticizing yourself about how it's going. Just put words on a page. For painters, work in the feverish frenzy of a Jackson Pollock. For musicians, it would be about improvisation.

You silence your inner critic, you don't plan for how you want things to go, you allow yourself to be derailed or distracted, and you trust that you'll end up where you need to be. Trust and faith are the two primary components of this card. Trust and faith in yourself, in your collaborators or peers, in the process. Where you were once controlling, you need to become flexible. Where you were once anxious, you need to become playful.

Just don't let your optimism shade into naivete. The Fool is not a great person to be when you are signing contracts, right? The French "art brut" painter Séraphine Louis is an example of all that is good and bad about the Fool. Art brut is definitely the Fool's realm, made as it is by outsiders to the art world, the self-taught, the mad, and the institutionalized. Séraphine created her transcendent, beautiful paintings of trees and flowers up in her attic, without any formal training and with no intent to do anything with the work after it was done. She couldn't really even afford much paint, working as she did as a domestic. When she ran out of money for supplies, Louis created her own paints from candle wax, from flowers and berries she picked in the wild, even from wine and blood. She painted because she loved to, and no one else in the world painted the way she did.

But Séraphine was a bit touched, and when people saw her work and wanted to buy it, she was so excited that she didn't think about the consequences. She did not think about fair compensation or how long they might stay interested; she took whatever was offered. And she spent that money immediately, without any thought to the future. Her end, in 1942 at the age of seventy-eight, was pretty much what you would expect.

One should emulate the Fool in creative pursuits, but still be ruthless when it comes time to sign a piece of paper.

RECOMMENDED MATERIALS

Tree of Paradise, painting by Séraphine Louis

Giant Steps, recording by John Coltrane

Les Champs Magnétiques, book by André Breton and
Philippe Soupault

THE MAGICIAN.

⤚ THE MAGICIAN – I ⤛

The Magician stands with representations of the four elements—the Cup, the Sword, the Coin, the Wand—lying before him on a table. The Magician has one arm raised toward the heavens and points down at the earth with the other.

The Magician is the creator, but whatever he writes, he is simply taking dictation from the heavens. He is the conduit rather than the source. He takes what is given to him by the divine (the arm gesturing up) and gives it form on the earth (the arm gesturing down). The Magician is given the number one, and so, like the Aces and the Fool, is another card that represents a new beginning.

The Magician is the card of creativity, of productivity, of everything that we hope to receive when we consult the deck about a problem with our project. It says the muses are present, you have everything you need, things will flow, birds will sing, and everything will work out oh so nicely.

Kind of, but also yes.

The Magician is a conduit. The muses, the gods, your unconscious—who cares about the source, because things are working! You seem to work effortlessly, you're in some kind of magical zone where you translate inspiration into words, music, movement, without even thinking about it. You get out of your own way, and the work just flows.

So the Magician cues us about a few different things. First, that we are ready to begin. Overpreparation is often procrastination disguised. "Oh, I am definitely going to write that book, but first I need to find the right notebook." Or "Before I can get started on that painting, it turns out I really need to read this giant stack of art theory and history books. It's totally necessary." The Magician says, "You're ready to work. Get to it."

Second, you need to become a conduit. If you mess with the process too much, if you try to strong-arm your own material, you're wasting your time and energy. Our expectations for a project do not always line up with what is actually best for the project, so if you're thinking, "No, this novel definitely needs to follow this super-rigid structure of five acts, five scenes per act," but the book itself wants to show up as a big, fluid, flowy, tidal kind of thing, then the hindrance here is *you*.

This is not about painstaking work, something labored over. The less control you have over it, the better. William Shakespeare was an incredibly fast writer, and if you look at the short period of time in which he wrote his many plays and sonnets, it will probably make you weep over how long it took you to write just your Twitter bio. He, of course, did not have the luxury of fussing over every word. If he did not write, he was not paid.

But his work has that remarkable rhythm and flow, as if he were simply taking divine dictation. Shakespeare became the conduit, for histories he had learned, stories he had heard, and he managed to convey them without interfering with them too much. (Which basically means that he stole a great deal from other storytellers, including their plotlines and characters, but he turned them into something so singular no one really cares anymore.)

Shakespeare was the supreme Magician, but we can't all be Shakespeare. It's hard even to think that we have anything to learn from Shakespeare; it's not like there is any advice that will turn you from you into him. But we can learn just to get to work, stop fussing, see where things go. Take the urges of the Fool and turn them into real, focused work.

RECOMMENDED MATERIALS

The Tempest, play by William Shakespeare

The Juggler, painting by Marc Chagall

The paintings of Hilma af Klint

⸻ THE HIGH PRIESTESS – II ⸻

A woman dressed in robes is seated. In her arms is a book or maybe a scroll. It is not only closed but also locked. Her foot rests on a crescent moon, and behind her stand one black pillar and one white pillar.

In the ancient world, the Priestesses tended the temples, led rites, and were taught the esoteric mysteries. Her card represents wisdom, secrets, and ritual. She is given the number two.

The High Priestess is about wisdom and knowledge. Knowledge for its own sake, not project-driven research or facts and figures you'll cram in there to make yourself sound smart. This is a card about input, not output.

The High Priestess cues us to when we need to feed our minds, our souls, our senses. Do you know that maxim "Write what you know"? Nonsense. That saying lets us off the hook for our more narcissistic impulses and for not trying to understand the world around us. The more a person learns—and this does not mean you need to get a PhD before you can work, merely that you nurture your curiosity and imagination—the more nuanced and complex his or her work becomes.

Think of the bardic system of the Celts. A poet was expected to learn everything—from myth and history to the natural world and science to art—before he was allowed to put pen to paper. Or, since this was still a time of an oral tradition, before he was allowed to perform his own work. A person with limited experience and knowledge was considered to be of limited talent and potential. By building up this great wealth of learning, the bards could work from a much larger resource.

An artist should always be learning. And not with any end result in mind, just guided by his or her curiosity. It doesn't even have to show explicitly in the work. Think of a writer such as P. L. Travers, who created the iconic character Mary Poppins in 1934. She was a student of mythology and fairy tales, studying with masters around the world. Travers wears that learning with a light touch in her children's books, but it's certainly one reason why her eccentric nanny became such an archetypal figure in literature.

Another example is Silvina Ocampo, a woman who used her wide knowledge of history, art, and mythology in her short stories and poetry. Her metaphysical learning puts her on par with William Blake and Jorge Luis Borges for the ability to create visionary work, but it's never showy. Learning has to be digested and incorporated, otherwise a writer just regurgitates it onto the page without any flair. Blake also drew from mythological and religious learning to create entirely new, mysterious, and bizarre visual worlds in his painting.

There's a touch of the mystical to the High Priestess, and artists under her sway tend to be a little kooky: Blake, Borges, Ocampo, Calvino, Carrington, Travers, the British poets Ted Hughes and Robert Graves, and dozens of others. They understand symbolism and metaphor, and so their work takes on a depth and layered quality that rewards multiple reading and viewing.

When the High Priestess shows up in a reading, it can indicate a need for you to put aside the work for a moment and make more time for study. If the card falls in a more active position, it might mean that it's time for you to draw on that knowledge you've already acquired. Either way, it's a card that draws your attention inward, rather than back to the page.

RECOMMENDED MATERIALS

The Topless Tower, book by Silvina Ocampo

What the Bee Knows: Reflections on Myth, Symbol, and Story, book by P. L. Travers

Mules and Men, book by Zora Neale Hurston

The Great Red Dragon and the Woman Clothed with the Sun, painting by William Blake

THE EMPRESS.

⸱⬦⸱ THE EMPRESS – III ⸱⬦⸱

A woman, often depicted as pregnant, sits in a lush garden.

The Empress is the combination of Venus—the lover—and the Moon—the mother. She is a sensual yet nurturing force. Her pregnancy signals her fertility and her potential for creation. The Empress represents the emotional world, the sensual world, and the possibility of new life. She is given the number three.

The Empress represents creative fertility; a tremendous potential to take an idea and turn it into a finished product. When we use motherhood metaphors to explain the creative process—nurturing an idea, pregnant with the project, birthing a book, that sort of thing—we're dealing with the Empress.

Do you know those wonderful polymaths who always seem to be doing one thing and then another? Someone like Madame

Anne-Louise-Germaine de Staël, who in the late seventeen hundreds and early eighteen hundreds hosted a literary salon and hung out with the great minds of her generation, wrote novels and essays and works of philosophy, opposed Emperor Napoléon I of France politically, and so on. Or around the same time, in Germany, Johann Wolfgang von Goethe, who studied botany, wrote plays, poetry, and novels, and served as a diplomat—along with drawing and producing scientific papers on the side. Such multitalented individuals don't do all of this strictly to make us feel inadequate, but because they are bursting with energy and know what to do with it.

The Empress is well centered. She is in many ways a combination of the two cards before her, the Magician and the High Priestess. She is balanced between intake and output, and she knows how to foster her imagination, as well as how to really get to work. In contrast with the Emperor, who follows, it's less about creating a legacy than it is about personal expression. She's very emotional, going back to her roots as a mother figure or a pregnant woman. So it's about an emotional, personal attachment to the work you're producing, rather than, "Well, if I want that building named after me when I'm dead, I had better finish writing this eight-volume history of the Counter-Reformation."

The tricky thing with the Empress is that, when stressed or upside down, she can be all potential. As in, it can be a little easy to get stuck in the pregnancy part and forget to actually give birth. And if she's too easily distracted, she can be overwhelmed with one idea after another, without giving enough time or focus to see any of them to completion.

But when you feel like you can't get anything done and the

Empress shows up, she's hinting that maybe you should try to take on more rather than focus on a smaller number of projects. The Empress is nothing if not fecund—she doesn't have only a rose garden but also tulips and fruit-bearing trees and a vegetable garden and some herbs and on and on. You might have hidden talents, you might have a capacity that is so much larger than you ever would have expected, and the only way you'll ever know is if you try.

RECOMMENDED MATERIALS

Venetian Epigrams, book by Johann Wolfgang von Goethe

"Feeling Good," recording by Nina Simone

Silueta series, photography by Ana Mendieta

THE EMPEROR.

THE EMPEROR – IV

A man sits on a throne in a sparse setting. His throne is often decorated with rams' heads.

The Emperor represents order and power. He is the patriarch, and so his concern is with establishing a foundation for not only his own work but also that of generations to come. He takes full responsibility for his actions. He provides structure. He is represented by the number four.

Where the Empress is soft, the Emperor is strong. Where the Empress is emotional, the Emperor is detached. He wants to maintain order, and he is building something that is going to take the next fifty years to manifest. He is patient and forward looking, because where the Empress wants to express herself, the Emperor wants to gain power.

This might sound a bit icky to some of you. You might not want to admit to yourself that you wish to dominate and control. You might think it's gross to mix power and art. But someone's gotta win the Nobel Prize every year, right? And to have that as a goal—not just the ego gratification part of it but also the achieving excellence part of it—is not a terrible thing.

Consider the Emperor to be the Germany card. Contemporary Germany, not . . . you know. The trains run on time, there is an order to things, there is a focus on planning for the future of both its citizens and its economy, there is a sense of logic and reason to the decisions the government makes. The Emperor doesn't have to be rapacious, taking from others to add to what it has already, which is more of a Seven of Swords or the Devil kind of thing. It's about tending to its own state in a reasonable way.

Using that energy creatively, we might think of the Emperor as being someone like the British writer C. S. Lewis. He plotted out the Chronicles of Narnia, finding the orderly structure to the seven books before he started work. Unlike other multiple-volume stories, the tone and the structure remain consistent throughout, because the series, published from 1950 to 1956, was planned so carefully. There are no wobbly to-and-fro plotlines like on the long-running television show *Lost*, which was clearly made up as it went along. Instead, Narnia was based on Lewis's deep learning of Greek and Roman mythology as well as Christian theology and fairy tales, and it functions both as adventure and as allegory.

Lewis is also a suitable Emperor figure because he was the chair of the literature department at Cambridge University. Emperors think in terms of career; they do not up and move from project to project. Everything builds on what came before it. Teaching is a fitting job for the Emperor, because he can spread his influence and leave a lasting legacy through his students.

The Emperor might seem conservative to some. Stability is important, rather than spontaneity and experimentation. But stability has its place alongside spontaneity and experimentation. There's a sense of lineage here, of working within an already established tradition. He is well complemented by the Fool, however. The Fool, or jester, traditionally acted out the mirth that the king or other leader was not allowed to. He was like the Emperor's shadow. Together they make a powerful alliance, with the Emperor trying to establish longevity, and the Fool bringing in light and humor. The Emperor paired with other heavy, traditional cards, however, could indicate that you're thinking too much about what you'll leave behind and not enough about what you should be doing now. Too much Emperor, and you can become so rigid that if you topple over, you'll shatter into a million pieces.

RECOMMENDED MATERIALS

The Chronicles of Narnia, book series by C. S. Lewis

Carnegie Libraries Across America, book by Theodore Jones

THE HIEROPHANT

·•· THE HIEROPHANT – V ·•·

A religious figure sits in his ceremonial vestments. He bestows the Pope's blessing upon the unseen congregation: first three fingers up, last two fingers down. The crossed keys represent the keys to heaven.

The Hierophant is given the number five, which is the number of completion. He is a five in perfect balance: all four elements—water, earth, air, fire—combined with the fifth, spirit. He calls us to be our higher selves, to find a perfect balance and lead others to their own.

The Hierophant is another name for the Pope. Don't worry, you don't have to take up religion when you get this card. It is more about becoming a leader, thinking outside your own concerns, and doing what is best for a community. You know how some athletes, musicians, and celebrities get caught up with drugs or the law, and

48

then, when their fans express disappointment, they say, "I never asked to be a role model"? This card is the opposite of that.

The Hierophant asks us to be better. Not just better, but the most balanced, the most compassionate, the most enlightened version of ourselves. It sounds nice, right? Who doesn't want to be his or her highest self? That's what we think until it comes time to actually do it, which means we have to stop grumbling, find two socks that match, stop eating potato chips, and start devoting ourselves selflessly to a cause.

You become your highest self by blending the four elements of the tarot deck—Cups (emotions), Wands (passion), Swords (intellect), and Coins (pragmatism)—with a sense of spirituality. You can substitute morality here if you like. You remove your own private concerns because there's simply no room for them. It's a bit like the detachment taught in Buddhism or the denial of the ego in Christianity. When we let the ego rule, we get stuck with the Devil, who is ten cards up at number fifteen. Here you put aside your own needs and work from a place of virtue. That's how you become a leader.

That does not mean you stop being a human being. Dr. Martin Luther King Jr. is an excellent example of the Hierophant. He knew that by becoming a visible, vocal figurehead of the civil rights movement he would be a target of the FBI, racist loonies, and hate organizations. And yet he continued to put himself in danger year after year because he was on a mission greater than himself.

Dr. King's writings still resonate, and they still inspire groups who are struggling for equal rights all over the world. His work transcended his human life.

Complications arise, however, when the Hierophant becomes powerful, as many great leaders can attest. With power comes the temptation to abuse that power and to use it thoughtlessly. And so King succumbed from time to time, to affairs with other women and so on. That does not diminish his greatness—mostly because he did not allow that side of him to go wild. But certainly other religious and social leaders (insert any number of politicians or religious leaders caught sexting, embezzling, or getting violent here) were not so disciplined.

When the Hierophant shows up, we need to question whether we need to step up as a leader in some way, whether we need to become active in a cause, whether we can be of service to something. It's also about coming together as a group to create something larger than ourselves. Find a way in your work to be of service to a greater good and find it in you to unearth your higher self.

RECOMMENDED MATERIALS

Calvary, film directed by John Michael McDonagh

A Call to Conscience: The Landmark Speeches of Dr. Martin Luther King Jr., book edited by Clayborne Carson and Kris Shepard

The Essential Rosa Luxemburg (Reform or Revolution and *The Mass Strike)*, book by Rosa Luxemburg

THE LOVERS – VI

Two figures, a man and a woman, either in an embrace or standing side by side.

This card is a divine calling, whether it depicts the Bible's Adam and Eve, or Psyche and Eros from Greek mythology. The two figures are drawn together not by choice but by a power greater than themselves. The card can represent love and desire, but it can also represent being taken over by an unknown power. The Lovers is number six.

I have a secret for you: the Lovers is kind of a terrible card. I know! Everyone loves this card, everyone wants this card, everyone is so very happy when it shows up in his or her future. Who doesn't want this wild, uncontrollable kind of love?

Well, everyone in the Greek mythological realm, for starters. The gods and goddesses were terrified of Eros. All it took was one prick of his arrow, and suddenly you were in love with a cow, telling all of your friends not to judge you: "You don't know this cow like I know this cow. This cow and I are in love." Eros could completely upend your life. Because the Lovers is not the cozy on-the-couch kind of love, with popcorn and Netflix and woolen socks. The Lovers is not your husband. It is the man you cry over once your husband has fallen asleep.

In our creative context, the Lovers is a calling. You've been pricked by an arrow, and now you are totally derailed. It's that moment of realization—"Oh God, I'm a poet, I'm an artist, I'm a fashion designer" (whatever)—and now you have to spend the rest of your life pursuing that identity relentlessly, not even letting poverty or obscurity or repeated failure deter you.

Perhaps the greatest depiction of this calling is Henry James's 1890 novel *The Tragic Muse*. Because James does not sugarcoat it. Once Nick Dormer, his protagonist, realizes he's actually a painter, it ruins his life. His family was ready to see him off into a career of politics, his fiancée suddenly realizes she has zero interest in being married to a penniless artist and leaves him, and he has to wave good-bye to a financially and socially secure life where everything is comfortable and expected. It's terrible.

But also thrilling, and James is good at managing the mix. There are things that fall away—that *must* fall away—when you devote yourself to a pursuit. Your family's approval cannot matter to you; you might have to decide between loneliness and security. There's no guarantee it will ever be worth it. You're going to have to ask yourself how much you want this. And do you really feel called strongly enough to bear all of the consequences?

Thematically, though, the Lovers is still about connection.

Connection that does not require alteration. Think of *The Lion in Winter*: two figures so in love they are out to destroy the other. It's about passion, about allowing yourself to be overwhelmed, allowing a love to be feral without needing to domesticate it. Loving something or someone for what or who it is, not what you want it to be. That takes an enormous amount of strength and integrity.

Which ties back in with the calling: allowing something to be scary, to be overwhelming; to devote yourself to it even if it requires great changes from you. It's something we have to live up to; it does not arrive neatly wrapped up in an understandable package. That would be easy. And the Lovers is always hard.

RECOMMENDED MATERIALS

The Tragic Muse, book by Henry James
Psyche Revived by Cupid's Kiss, sculpture by Antonio Canova
Hedwig and the Angry Inch, film directed by
John Cameron Mitchell

THE CHARIOT – VII

The charioteer stands in his chariot, which is pulled by two animals. Common versions of the card have the Chariot pulled by two horses, two swans, or two sphinxes. One animal is black; the other white. Often there are no reins, implying a lack of control over the animals. And yet the charioteer seems unconcerned by this.

One of the more complicated cards in the Major Arcana, the Chariot represents paradox, the battle between the ego and the unconscious, and the tension of opposites. But rather than having the charioteer torn in half by two opposite desires, he uses that tension to propel himself and his chariot forward. The Chariot is given the number seven.

At its core, the Chariot represents victory. Victory over difficult circumstances, over your peers and competitors, over your own low expectations. The Chariot is the part of us that wants to win.

Now, winning and creativity can seem like a bad pairing, and indeed, they often go wrong. Some people put so much focus and energy into grabbing the big prize, they forget that after the champagne and sequined gowns have been discarded, they still have to go back to work the next day. The puffed-up ego can take over, and it can demolish your work ethic. (See: the out-of-control Oscar campaigns; see also: the Oscar curse that can end careers.)

But a healthy ego, engaged in a kind of friendly rivalry with those of one's peers, can push an artist to do better, do more, try harder—just as an unfriendly rivalry can lock two brilliant minds in an airless chamber, until their mutual hatred and sense of competitiveness destroy their ambitions and their character.

On the side of the friendly rivalry, we have Pablo Picasso and Henri Matisse, two wildly different artists. Where Picasso was masculine, Matisse was feminine. Where Picasso was cerebral, Matisse was emotional. Where Picasso was intricate and elaborate, Matisse was simple and refined. And when they were first introduced to each other's work, they both thought, "Nonsense." But eventually the two engaged in a bit of a competition; they would sometimes paint the same subject from their different viewpoints and methods, and debate whose was better. They disagreed, but they studied each other's work and learned from each other.

Compare that to the writers Norman Mailer and Gore Vidal, who took literal swings at each other on occasion. They engaged in conversation only to trade insults, and they didn't read each other's work carefully but looked at it only to find ways to take it apart. Neither grew from the experience, and both writers suffered in their work when they became too dominated by their egos. Both decayed into writing bloated texts that few could engage with, each a hero in his own mind.

Now, the Chariot is not only about competition and victory, although that is a large part of it. It's also about paradox and gaining control over one's unconscious impulses. Part of the card is about using both the ego and the unconscious together to drive us toward our goals, gaining mastery over any of the darker impulses, any self-destructiveness or narcissistic indulgences. You can see how both Matisse and Picasso, able to use their opposite as a kind of inspiration rather than as an enemy, controlled their need to destroy each other. Victory does not have to mean the total annihilation of your competitor; it can also mean elevating him or her as well. Vidal and Mailer were not so self-aware.

So make sure that your need to win is rooted in your need for self-improvement and recognition, and is not coming from some kind of twisted bloodlust. Competition can be as inspiring as it is degrading.

RECOMMENDED MATERIALS

Matisse and Picasso: The Story of Their Rivalry and Friendship, book by Jack Flam

Amadeus, film directed by Milos Forman

Writing Dangerously: Mary McCarthy and Her World, book by Carol Brightman

STRENGTH – VIII

A woman is calmly petting a lion next to her. She is not overpowering the lion, nor is either the woman or the lion injured.

Strength is not about brute force, it is instead about the strength of patience, of receptivity, of innocence. The woman on the card waited a long time for the lion to trust her, so she has endurance. She also has compassion for the beast and gazes down upon it with love. The Strength card can be either the number eight or the number eleven, depending on the deck you use.

There are times when we need to get on our horse, grab our weaponry, and hunt down that thing we want. All of that exciting Knight energy: "I want that, so I'll go off and clobber it and drag it back." That kind of stuff.

Then there are the times when we need Strength, which is get-

57

ting what we want by standing perfectly still, by being open and receptive, and by daring to be vulnerable. We want the lion to come sit in our lap, and so we will sit very quietly and wait for it. We can't overpower it, we can't force it to do what we want, so we will sit here patiently, calmly until the lion feels safe enough to approach.

Strength is a card of endurance. You show your strength through weathering difficult circumstances and by outlasting the fear that tells you, "This is never going to work; you should give up and go home." It's a quiet resolve dependent on your capacity for empathy and kindness.

In the story of how the fourteenth-century Persian poet Hafiz came to his poetic powers, there was a local legend that anyone who kept vigil at the tomb of a master poet who had died years before—a forty-day vigil without sleep—would be granted the gift of poetry and their heart's desire. Hafiz kept that vigil, despite numerous temptations, despite exhaustion and despair. When he was granted the gift of poetry and asked what his heart's desire was, all earthly concerns fell away, and he answered, "Knowledge of God." By which he meant not just religious knowledge but also knowledge of his own True Self.

Strength is not an easy card, because we're usually not sure what we want. What do you want from your creative endeavors? Self-expression? Fame? Acceptance by the elite? Wisdom? Perhaps you think you want wisdom, and you believe you have the patience to sit quietly and wait for it, but as soon as someone offers you a magazine cover and a Channing Tatum film adaptation, you think, "Oh, I was wrong. It turns out this is what I wanted all along. I was just confused."

To be clear on your goals and your desires, and then to have the endurance to wait for those things to come to you, is not an easy task. This is about patience, not about procrastination or passivity. For Hafiz, his knowledge of God and his own self took another forty years of learning and study; it was not bestowed upon him immediately, as the language of poetry had been. Proving wisdom is another thing worth waiting for quietly: while our ability to express something might come early on in the process—our technical skills with words, paint, and so on—having something worth expressing often comes much later in the process.

RECOMMENDED MATERIALS

The Gift, book of poetry by Hafiz
Survival in Auschwitz, book by Primo Levi
Dialogue with Death, book by Arthur Koestler

THE HERMIT.

❧ THE HERMIT – IX ❧

A man stands, cloaked, holding a lamp in his hand to guide his way. His long beard and old age suggest that he has not had human company for some time.

The Hermit represents social isolation, in both its benefits and its detriments. Isolation can bring clarity, peace, and meditation. But it can also make us lonely and eccentric. Both outcomes are possible with this card. The Hermit is given the number nine.

Sometimes it is important to get away, shut yourself off from noise, stop asking for other people's input, and do the work you want to do.

This isn't about the noise of the internet, about social media, about wasting your productivity on checking email instead of doing creative work. Although yes to all of that, do try to find a space outside of that buzz. This is more about moving away from the collective, having the confidence in your own work to stand on your own, and no longer being swayed by other people's opinions of what you should do.

Certainly we benefit at times from an outsider perspective. When we work in a group or collaborate with a partner, we get vital information and inspiration. But sometimes those voices can lead us astray. Someone will say something negative about what you are doing, that comment sticks in your head, and all of a sudden you are ready to make drastic changes just to please someone else.

The Hermit asks us to pull away from outside influences. The artists Claude Cahun and Marcel Moore had a strong community of collaborators, partners, and peers in Paris between the wars. This tight-knit group of artists, writers, theater folk, and musicians influenced one another heavily, working together constantly and sharing ideas. But Cahun and Moore wanted to pull away a bit; try something different. And so they moved to Jersey Island, located in the English Channel separating France and England.

There they began collaborating on strange, beautiful photographs. They were a long series of self-portraits of Cahun—Marcel worked the camera—that predated the work of artists such as the Mexican painter Frida Kahlo and the American conceptual photographer Cindy Sherman. Outside the influence of the Paris cabal, they found a purer voice; a more authentic way of working. They weren't totally alone—they had each other—but they were isolated socially and physically from the art world. So much so that their work was not discovered or displayed until after their deaths.

Pulling the Hermit doesn't mean you have to go build a cabin in the woods, although if you've had the impulse to do it, why not?

But it does mean that perhaps you need to shore up your boundaries a bit and make sure you're not taking on too many other people's opinions as your own.

On the flip side, the Hermit card originates with the story of Diogenes, the ancient Greek philosopher who went out with his lantern, looking for one honest man. He never found one, of course. We all lie, we all cheat in our ways. If one has taken the Hermit too far, you might find yourself isolated like Diogenes, with standards so high that not a single human being on the planet (including yourself) could clear them. Make sure your isolation has not turned into stubborn arrogance. If you think no one knows better than you about *anything*, you probably need to start thinking a little less of yourself and a little more of others.

RECOMMENDED MATERIALS

The photography of Claude Cahun and Marcel Moore
Gravity and Grace, book by Simone Weil
Walden, book by Henry David Thoreau

WHEEL ᴏꜰ FORTUNE.

THE WHEEL OF FORTUNE - X

The Wheel of Fortune depicts just that: a large, spinning wheel. Some cards show the wheel with figures being tossed off as it turns; others show no people on the card at all, to depict our lack of control over it. Some cards show four figures in the corners, representing the four authors of the Gospels.

The Wheel of Fortune is about fate, about the things we cannot control, and about luck—both good and bad. It is where our free will ends. It reminds us that while we might be on top of the world now, things can change, and we can always end up in the gutter. And if we are in the gutter, it reminds us that it is possible for things to improve. It is the number ten.

We have absolutely zero control over so much of our lives and our careers, and that is indicated by the Wheel of Fortune. Herman

Melville and Vincent van Gogh were geniuses, but no one recognized that until after they were long dead; others are mediocre at best, but they seem to get all of the good jobs and attention because they knew the right people or were born into the right family. We can call it fate, luck, coincidence, but whatever the mechanism is, it's beyond our control.

And so the Wheel of Fortune asks us to contemplate the divide between our sense of free will and our "fate"—and *fate* here just means everything that is immune to our will, that we can't force. There are demands on your time, there are circumstances such as your financial situation and your home life, and much of that is nonnegotiable. How you respond to those circumstances, though, has to do with your sense of free will. All you have today is fifty-eight cents, an orange, and some pencils: What can you do with that? Today you have forty minutes between coming home from work and the moment your children return from school: What can you do with that?

The rest of it you have to get over. You can build up a lot of bitterness about the unfairness of life. Yes, life is unfair. No, we do not live in a meritocracy. You can be brilliant and never see the rewards of that. You read these stories all the time about models who are discovered at the grocery store by agents and are whisked off to become international superstars. The singer Tim Booth was discovered not for his singing but because of the way he was dancing at a club. As a result, he came to front the British pop band James, which became wildly successful in the 1990s. These little coincidences and accidents of fate can drive you mad if you are not the beneficiary of them. It's not like you can troll grocery stores forever, sucking in your cheeks and posing nonchalantly, hoping an agent will pass by. Eventually you're going to have to buy something or they'll ask you to leave.

The only thing you can really do is concentrate on what is within your control. You can push the boundaries of that by doing all of the things you are supposed to do, such as learning to network and joining up with peers to share stories and tips. You can also help out others in need. Are you a writer with a lot of brilliant friends who can't seem to get published? Pool your resources and start a small publishing company. Want to use your artistic skills, but no one will ask? There are public art projects, there are nonprofits for disadvantaged children that would probably love an art instructor, and so on.

There is an element of karma at play with this card. Not in the sense that if you are super good you will be rewarded for it. (See above regarding the bad news of not living in a meritocracy.) It's how you choose to respond to circumstances and limitations that will define you as a person. So you can grumble softly to yourself all day long about how you are an undiscovered genius, why can't anyone see that, and you can yell at your television when someone less talented than you is being given some big prize. Or you can use that energy for something creative rather than something destructive.

RECOMMENDED MATERIALS

Moby-Dick, book by Herman Melville
Sunflowers, painting by Vincent van Gogh
"Sit Down," recording by James

⊶ JUSTICE – XI ⊷

A woman with a serious expression holds an evenly balanced scale in one hand and a sword in the other. Sometimes she is blindfolded.

Justice is the courtroom, the binding contract, the karmic return. She is not fair, she is just, and knowing the difference between the two is the crux of this particular card. Justice requires an impersonal, abstract point of view when she shows up. In some decks, she is placed at number eight; in others, she is at number eleven.

Justice does not really give us something to do so much as a way to think. She requires emotional detachment, an airy overview, a way of examining what's going on without fear or anger. She asks us to put aside our more base nature and see things on a larger scale.

There are times when anger is useful. It can be energizing, it can be rousing. James Baldwin's 1963 essay collection about civil rights and American racism, *The Fire Next Time*, is a good example of this. It is furious, and it is righteous. It speaks to a large population's frustrations, and it can inspire people to act and speak out.

But anger is not always appropriate, even if the source of inspiration is a gross injustice. Sometimes, in order to answer injustice, one must remain elevated, cool, and temperate. Otherwise, injustice can be met with even more injustice—an eye for an eye that can get out of hand. And that's Justice, who can see through the rage and yet still keep her head. Justice finds her way through the actions of nonviolent advocates such as Mohandas Gandhi and suffragette Alice Paul. The anger and despair at their situations might be present, but those feelings are put to the side in order to focus on progress.

It's like the split between the figure of Justice and what came before her, which was the Furies of Greek mythology. The Furies called out for revenge; if blood was spilt, they wanted to spill more blood to even things out. But the birth of Athena, the Greek goddess of wisdom, changed that, and instead of vengeance and feuds, a system of law and order came to be. It might not be as satisfying emotionally, but it prevents chaos from erupting.

The playwright and essayist Václav Havel used satire and philosophy to battle the oppressive Communist government of his Czechoslovakia. He used absurdity and peaceful protest where they used brutality and violence. He used grassroots communities to distribute his and other dissidents' samizdat—hand-copied and covertly circulated—writings, while the government tried to suppress them with power and control. And even when he had the opportunity to escape to the West, even after spending years in prison for his acts of resistance, he didn't take it. He did not care for his own safety as much as he cared for the safety of his fellow citizens.

Havel and the other dissidents were eventually successful in overthrowing the corrupt government, and in 1989 Havel took office as the country's first democratically elected president since the 1940s. His philosophical writings—about power, about dissent, about trying to live under oppressive circumstances—became influential and important in post–Communist Europe, but also his wise actions as president showed other nations how to transition to democracy and freedom.

Justice doesn't ask you only to examine your own life and work for its imbalances, it also asks you to look at society. Where is the system unfair? How are you participating in that inequality? It asks you to examine the larger structure to find your place in it and then figure out where you can take a stand.

RECOMMENDED MATERIALS

"To Those Who Follow in Our Wake," poem by Bertolt Brecht

Narrative of the Life of Frederick Douglass, An American Slave, book by Frederick Douglass

The Garden Party, play by Václav Havel

The Fire Next Time, book by James Baldwin

THE HANGED MAN.

ⵈ THE HANGED MAN – XII ⵈ

A man hangs upside down, either from a tree or from a post. He is suspended with a rope tied around his ankle. His legs are positioned with one knee straight and the other knee bent, to create a shape resembling an upside-down and inverted number four. His expression remains serene and his body language relaxed.

Along with the Chariot, this is one of the most complex cards in the Major Arcana. Sometimes the Hanged Man suggests that you need your world to go topsy-turvy before you can get a really good look at it. But the card also asks for contemplation over action; detachment over involvement. It's a time to reflect and accumulate information. It falls at number twelve in the series.

The Hanged Man is not as gruesome as it sounds. The man on the card is not dead, merely suspended upside down by one foot. And it's not as passive as it sounds. Oftentimes this card is dismissed as a time of limbo, a time of waiting. But more than anything, this is a card of the pursuit of wisdom.

Let's say that you have a revelation: that big "Oh, man!" moment where suddenly the whole world looks different to you, and everything makes a new kind of sense. That moment is preceded and proceeded by the Hanged Man. In order to get to that moment, something has to shake us out of our complacency; something that makes us question and seek a new answer. And then after our revelation, we need a moment to contemplate how this changes things for us.

It could be a family secret, like "Your father is not your real father." Suddenly you understand your place in your family differently and things that had bothered you for years, but you couldn't figure out why, make sense now. Or it could be a revelation about the work you're doing. Either way, the Hanged Man gives us a moment to contemplate and then incorporate that new information.

The Hanged Man is a pivot. Things were going one way, and now you're hanging back to gather the strength and energy to shift. Think of a ball thrown in the air. There's one brief moment where the ball seems to hang suspended, unmoving, as it runs out of energy upward and starts hurtling back downward. So while it might be in limbo in some sense, it doesn't mean that you can throw up your hands and say, "This isn't working, I'm going to the spa." It won't help to dispel the tension; you need the tension to propel you forward.

The Hanged Man is based on the story from Norse mythology of Odin learning the secret of the runes. Runes were an early form of written language, and so the story of their invention is the story of a pivot from oral culture to written culture. In the story, Odin, the supreme god and creator, hangs himself upside down from the Tree of Life for nine days. He pierces himself with a spear and allows much of his blood to drain away, until he is suspended not only between the earth and the air but also between life and death. At that point, he receives the gift of understanding the runes, which gives him a kind of magical power over reality.

You can see what a complex card this is. There's the idea of sacrifice, of transition, of a new kind of understanding. Odin had to reach a meditative state to gain his knowledge, and in order to do that, he had to strip away all that was unnecessary—in his case, that included a great deal of blood and almost his life. It's also about submitting yourself to the task at hand, being patient and allowing your project to reveal its secrets to you, rather than always trying to get your own way.

Which does not mean that you have to stop eating for a week and wander through the desert while taking hallucinogenic drugs until your art starts speaking to you. (Although if that is what you want, I am not going to try to stop you.) But maybe what you're trying to do is not what should be done, and in order to understand that, you're going to have to take a break, turn yourself upside down, and surrender yourself to what is revealed.

In some versions of the Odin story, the shapes of the runes revealed themselves in the shapes made by nature: cranes flying through the sky, the branches of the trees as they moved in the wind, the blades of grass, and so on. By taking the time to notice small things, to stop thinking so much and stop trying to control so much, he could finally see the bigger picture.

RECOMMENDED MATERIALS

The Alphabet Versus the Goddess: The Conflict Between Word and Image, book by Leonard Shlain

D'Aulaires' Book of Norse Myths, book by Ingri and Edgar d'Aulaire

The "Oh my God, my whole marriage has been a lie" fireside chapter of *The Portrait of a Lady*, book by Henry James

⊶ DEATH – XIII ⊷

The imagery of this card changes from deck to deck more than perhaps any other, depending on the artist's particular feelings and interpretations of death. It could be the Grim Reaper, an Ophelia-like woman, an angel of mercy, or something more gruesome.

Death indicates an end of something. It is not essentially good or bad; it is valueless. The something that is ending could be something wonderful or something terrible. The end could bring pain or relief. But Death is a definite end, not something that can be salvaged or negotiated with. Death falls at the number thirteen.

While the Death card does not mean the obvious—you are totally going to die this week (unless you forward this tarot card to seven friends in the next twenty-four hours)—it is an ending. Death has a tendency to show up at the end of relationships, the end of jobs, anytime you transition into a new identity or stage of life. It has shown up once or twice for my clients right before weddings, which tends to freak out the brides. But, I point out, your life as a single woman is dying, and a new way of being is beginning, so the card is appropriate. Just not the cheeriest of messengers.

The Death card must be respected because the transformation he is marking is deep and meaningful. A part of you or your life has to die so that something new can be born. (Or maybe a project that isn't working out has to be left to die so new work can begin.) We can often cling to old ways of thinking or living, not because it serves us but because we don't like uncertainty.

But just because something isn't good for us doesn't mean that we don't mourn its absence. We can become nostalgic about eras that were actually pretty terrible to live through: Victorian England might have had nice dresses, but it was a really good time only if you were a white man with a lot of money. That's one of the negative aspects of the Death card—remembering something as better than it was. Or seeing whatever replaces it as being inherently inferior, because it does not line up with what was lost.

Death has been the muse for many an artist. Just search Google Images for "Death of Ophelia." Artists from John Everett Millais to Eugène Delacroix to Alexandre Cabanel have captured the iconic image of the maiden drowning in the stream. The Romantics, from the poets to the painters, used death to inspire their odes, paintings, even their fashion. And nobody turned mourning into high art quite like the designers of Victorian mourning garments. From the shoes to the jewelry to the elaborate dresses, death became very chic.

Then there's the story of the unknown woman who drowned in

the River Seine and became immortalized in many artistic renderings. She was a real woman who either fell in the water or committed suicide, and her angelic-looking death mask became a source of inspiration for artists and writers throughout Paris. They speculated on what would lead a woman to such a drastic act, and they imagined her life through song and story. She was the subject of a Rainer Maria Rilke novel, a poem by Vladimir Nabokov, a short story by Hungarian playwright Ödön von Horváth, and many others.

Death allows us to bid farewell to the way we were working or living before, and that change can have great inspirational impact on us.

RECOMMENDED MATERIALS

The Last September, book by Elizabeth Bowen
The Siege of Krishnapur, book by J. G. Farrell
Ophelia, painting by John Everett Millais

·-· TEMPERANCE – XIV ·-·

A figure stands at a river, mixing two cups. One is filled with hot water, the other cold water. The figure has one foot in the river, one foot on the ground. In contemporary decks, the figure is often portrayed as an angel; traditionally, however, it is not an angel but a hermaphrodite.

Temperance is about blending two extremes, or two opposites, to create something new. The hot and cold water combines in her cups to create something temperate. The male and female bodies are combined to create the hermaphrodite. There is also a sense of hanging back here, of waiting to see what the river will bring to us as it flows. Temperance is represented by the number fourteen.

Temperance is an easily misunderstood card, as it has become associated mostly with abstention. Not drinking, not participating, denying yourself something. But that breaks away from the origins of the card, which traditionally portrays a hermaphrodite blending two cups of water—one hot and one cold—to create something in the middle between these two extremes.

Ovid's story of Hermaphroditus shows the child as the offspring of the Greek deities Hermes and Aphrodite. He was born a boy and was so beautiful that even a nymph, sworn to chastity and devotion to the Greek virgin moon goddess Artemis, flung herself at him. Her desire was so strong that they fused into one being, with the sexual characteristics of both male and female.

The theme, then, is not about abstention but about finding a middle way. It is about taking two opposites and creating something new.

There have been great androgynous women stars, from Marlene Dietrich in a tuxedo to Katharine Hepburn with her swagger and her trousers. Fewer male performers are willing to exhibit their feminine side. The stand-up comedian Eddie Izzard performed in dresses and heels, and the witty Irishman Oscar Wilde grew out his hair to scandalous lengths for his time, but it's been more socially acceptable for women to express masculinity than for men to express femininity.

The so-called glam rock of the early 1970s was an interesting gender-bending era, as men discovered the pleasures of sequins and feathers, eyeliner and lipstick. Musicians such as Marc Bolan of T. Rex, David Bowie, and Brian Eno of Roxy Music dressed up, flirted, and presented themselves in a feminine mode. It's a bit of a shame that the era ended.

If anything, the Temperance card argues against overcorrection—from veering from one extreme to another, like a person who has had a terrible diet for years, filling himself with junk food and beer, and then becomes a militant juice-fast follower and lectures others on how they need to leech out toxins. Or an atheist who converts immediately to a fundamentalist religious belief. Temperance asks you to find another way.

Wherever you are the most steadfast, wherever you are the most stubborn and rigid, that is where Temperance is asking you to reconsider your extreme position. If your work is too logical, maybe you need to spend some time with the surrealists. If your work is too minimalist, maybe it's time to explore decadence. If your work is too feminine, maybe it's time to pull out that tuxedo. That kind of painstaking rebalancing takes time and patience, because it's too easy to just grab the steering wheel and wrench it in the opposite direction.

RECOMMENDED MATERIALS

The Slider, recording by T. Rex
Orlando, film directed by Sally Potter
Una, Lady Troubridge, painting by Romaine Brooks
My Gender Workbook, book by Kate Bornstein

·-· THE DEVIL – XV ·-·

The crouching Devil mimics the stance of the Magician, but by pointing downward with one hand, a hand that is holding a lit torch, he sets fire to the tail of the man in front of him. There are two figures in chains at his feet, a man and a woman, like the couple on the Lovers card. The chains are loose around their necks and look as if they could easily be slipped off.

The Devil represents an out-of-control ego. Rather than being a conduit like the Magician, the Devil tries to push his own will for power and gain and self-destructs in the process. The man and woman, allowing themselves to be chained, show a willfulness to the behavior. The self-destruction could be stopped, but they are choosing not to. Sometimes this card indicates obsessive love, uncontrolled drinking or drug use, or untreated illness. The Devil is the number fifteen.

The traditional reading of the Devil is, "Hi, maybe you would like to stop drinking and drugging yourself to death, yeah?" It's the card of self-destruction, but there are all kinds of ways we can destroy ourselves.

Artists who rely on alcohol or drugs for their creative process often find themselves at the mercy of those substances. The Devil could represent all of the Twenty-seven Club, the long list of musicians and artists who died at the age of twenty-seven, mostly from the consequences of substance abuse: Jimi Hendrix, Janis Joplin, Jim Morrison, Jean-Michel Basquiat, Kurt Cobain, Amy Winehouse, and so on. It's a long list of talented, brilliant creators who got lost and couldn't find their way back home.

But on a larger scale, the Devil represents self-defeating behavior. We get stuck in destructive patterns, and we refuse to consider stopping. A lot of the time, that's because those patterns feel good. Booze and pills feel good; that's why people take them in the first place. But then they gain control over you, and stopping would mean relearning how to be creative, how to live soberly, even how to be around other people who don't abuse substances, and how to perform. It's not a journey a lot of people who get stuck are willing to take, and some of them die as a consequence.

It's not just addiction, however. Any type of obsessive behavior falls under the realm of the Devil. A love affair that you know is bad for you but you can't quite ever put an end to it. The voice in your head that says, "This is not good enough, you'll never be good enough, why even try?" Knowing that you're depressed or suffering from panic attacks and yet refusing to talk to someone about it. All of that eventually destroys productivity and your life.

The Devil can be a muse, but one that is hard to control. Certainly there is a lot of great literature and art about sexual obsession. Drugs have inspired great art—but don't do them, kids—from opium, to absinthe, to alcohol. And there are times when the Devil seems to reign, like in Weimar Berlin during the 1920s. Germany was in an economic and spiritual spiral after World War I, and yet it was a time of fruitful creativity, much of it focusing on ideas of darkness, deviance, and decadence.

The singer, actress, dancer, and writer Anita Berber was the epitome of Weimar Berlin. She danced naked, she appeared in films, she performed wild stage shows. She was publicly bisexual and paraded around her many lovers. It was shocking for the time, but she became a tremendous star. She indulged, wildly. Any type of alcohol, any type of drug. It should not be surprising that she died young, at the age of twenty-nine.

The Devil was certainly Berber's muse, and her work was widely influential. But, of course, it was not sustainable. The Devil does have creative power: to break taboos, to reveal the darker side of life, to show the pleasure of transgression. But one must not fall too deep if one hopes to recover. (Weimar Germany itself then fell hopelessly into Nazism and you know the rest.) A bit of the Devil is necessary for every creative genius; otherwise there's no depth, no sting to the work. A Devil-less existence would be a little too fluffy, a little too safe. But one must always know when to walk away.

RECOMMENDED MATERIALS

The Seven Addictions and Five Professions of Anita Berber:
   Weimar Berlin's Priestess of Depravity, book by Mel Gordon
The Jimi Hendrix Experience, recording by Jimi Hendrix
The Confessions of Noa Weber, book by Gail Hareven

THE TOWER.

THE TOWER - XVI

A tower, hit by lightning or perhaps simply on fire, is nearing collapse. In many versions of the card, two figures fall from the top of the tower to the ground below.

Rather than the self-destruction of the Devil, the Tower is destruction that comes from the outside. It is a shaking, a tumult, a calamity. What you have built up, the Tower takes down. It is perhaps the most dreaded card in the deck. It falls at number sixteen.

Okay, I can hear the wailing and see the hair-pulling from here. No card inspires dread quite like the Tower. All of that work—all of that fragile, beautiful, time-consuming work—gone to waste. The Tower is ruthless; it is the card of destruction and chaos. It takes your work and throws it out the window. Wail and pull your hair all you want, but there is no negotiating with this card.

Remember that scene in Louisa May Alcott's *Little Women*, where Amy throws Jo's stories into the fire? That's the feeling of the Tower: the realization that all is lost, and you will have to start over from the beginning. A friend's studio flooded during a hurricane, and she lost not only years of work but also all of her supplies. Everything was ruined and had to be tossed out; there was nothing left that was salvageable.

It does not have to be quite so literal. It could be a sudden realization that what you're working on is not any good. It could be a rejection from someone you had pinned a lot of hopes on. In whichever way the Tower manifests, the result is the same. You feel shaken, and you feel vulnerable.

Many artists throughout time have lost work to fire, flood, rejection, and disinterest. Then you have to decide—do you try again? Or do you cut your losses and start on something new? If you do try again, do you do it in the same way, or was there something wrong about it that caused the finger of God to come down and smite it? The Tower requires a lot of soul-searching, because it can be difficult to find the courage and the energy to carry on after such an incident.

Thematically, though, the Tower asks us: What needs to be destroyed in order to be rebuilt? Humans are so very resistant to change, it can take an outside force or a tragedy to force us to rethink things. The Tower could be revolution, such as the beheading of the corrupt aristocracy in eighteenth-century revolutionary France to bring about real political change. It could be the boos and riotous negativity that greeted Stravinsky's ballet *The Rite of Spring* at its first performance in 1913—the audience wanted something recognizable; something that sounded like something they had heard before.

If you need a cheerier face to put on the Tower, think of the fairy tale of Rapunzel. A witch has locked her up in that tower. She's not terribly unhappy with her circumstances, until she falls in love with the handsome prince. Then, of course, she wants more from her life. But she's stuck in that tower—what to do? First, she brings the handsome prince up into her tower, via her long hair, but that doesn't work. It infuriates the witch. And so she's tossed out of the tower, unwillingly, by the witch. She falls, it hurts, it's scary. Suddenly there's a whole world to deal with; not just the contents of her cell. But she had to be removed forcibly, because change and vulnerability are terrifying.

The Tower can be liberating, but only if we don't cling to what came before. Limitations can feel safe; doing things in the old way is comfortable and familiar. But it's okay to greet the card with dread, to wonder how much of your work it's going to take out when it shows up. But what it takes out, just wave good-bye to, and start to plan a life without it.

RECOMMENDED MATERIALS

Invasion 68: Prague, book of photography by Josef Koudelka
The Sun Also Rises, book by Ernest Hemingway
Achtung Baby, recording by U2

THE STAR - XVII

A naked woman kneels at a stream (or perhaps at the edge of a lake). She has two cups in her hands. She fills one with the water from the stream. With the other, she pours water back in. It is nighttime, and the stars are out.

After the darkness of the Devil and the Tower, the Star provides a respite, a time of rest and recovery. It indicates that you are exactly where you should be and doing exactly what you should be doing. You have reached a state of balance: for everything you take from the world, you give back in return. It also asks you to take care of your health. The Star finds itself at number seventeen.

The Star is all about orientation. We use the stars to guide us and to tell us where we are, where we are going. And so when it appears in a reading, it's a marker that it is time to think about how we are positioned in the world and how we would like to be.

In order to do that, though, we have to be entirely sure of who we are. If we are truly going to know where we want to end up, if we are truly going to know where on this planet we belong, then we have to be certain of our identity. We take on a lot of other people's desires and a lot of society's desires, because that is easy. So we start to think, "I need a nice house, I need a wife, I need a two-week vacation on a beach every year. If that is what makes everyone else happy, surely it'll make me happy, too."

In terms of creativity, we take on other creators' structures, their themes, their ideas. "Right now squids in space are doing really well at the box office; I definitely want to write a squid-in-space screenplay next!" Or "Everyone else is getting a master of fine arts degree; I must need to get an MFA, too. That will make me a better artist."

Breaking away from those conformities can be very difficult. You don't get a lot of company out in the wild. It can be harder for an audience to understand what you're doing. Also, it's not always easy to know what it is you want. First, you often have to go through a long list of things you thought you wanted and realize, "Nope, this doesn't work for me, either." It's a process.

But at the end of that process is the Star. Orientation. You figure out where you are, you figure out how to navigate your way to getting there. It's a card of healing, of feeling perfectly placed.

Think of it as the Ziggy Stardust card. David Bowie's first recordings are completely normal. They sound like every other middle-of-the-road musician at the time: boring and safe. It took a lot of guts to go from that to "Yeah, no, actually I'm from Mars;

I need to go buy some wigs." There was no guarantee that risk was going to pay off, but it was absolutely in keeping with who David Bowie was and is.

Also note that was not an individual move: Bowie had a long list of collaborators who helped him shape his stage persona, his costumes, his music. We not only found where he was in the world singularly, but he found his compatriots and supporters. That's another aspect of the Star card. When you start working in alignment with your own weirdo desires, other weirdos—the best kinds of weirdos—tend to find you.

So the Star asks you to be a freak, a misfit, a weirdo. It asks you to stop pretending to be a normal person with normal wants. None of us is normal. Coming after the Devil and the Tower, it's when you're so shaken and exhausted that you can't pretend anymore. Stripped of external methods of protection, you're vulnerable and absolutely true. The Star lets you rest, and you start to see the rewards of going through the difficult process of individuation.

RECOMMENDED MATERIALS

The Rise and Fall of Ziggy Stardust and the Spiders from Mars, recording by David Bowie

In Memoriam to Identity, book by Kathy Acker

Dead Ringers, film directed by David Cronenberg

THE MOON.

⋅·⊱ THE MOON – XVIII ⊰·⋅

The moon is full. At the water's edge, a lobster is crawling out of the water and onto land. There is a path marked out, but it is guarded by a wolf on one side and a dog on the other.

The Moon stands for all we cannot understand rationally: our unconscious desires, our dreams, our fears. It is our wild side; our fishy, intuitive side; the part of us that is still animal. It often shows up when we need to be paying attention to our dreams. It is positioned at number eighteen.

When we encounter the Moon, we have to let go of our rational selves for the time being. We have to let dreams, intuition, and emotions be our guide. Whatever happens with the Moon does not necessarily have to make sense; it's more about a feeling.

Many creators have worked with dream logic, from the writer

Italo Calvino to the filmmaker David Lynch. The nightmarish works of a painter like Francis Bacon haunt viewers long after they've turned away from the canvas. The entire surrealist movement could be said to be under the sway of the Moon, as many of them believed there was a kind of wisdom to be found in madness. "The realistic attitude," André Breton writes in *The Surrealist Manifesto*, "clearly seems to me to be hostile to any intellectual or moral advancement. I loathe it, for it is made up of mediocrity, hate, and dull conceit."

This is not entirely comfortable territory. It's the type of thing that divides audiences strongly. Some people love, fanatically, the dreamy, strange, unusual, and illogical movies that Lynch directs, like *Blue Velvet* and *Mulholland Drive*, with their odd imagery and twisty plotlines that don't really make sense. Other people hate them. Vociferously.

It's because it is difficult, as an audience member and as a creator, to try to stop making sense. The Moon rules our dreams, and that's a good way to think about this card. They don't make sense on a logical level, but on a personal level, on an emotional level, they do. The location in a dream will shift without warning; dead people walk beside the living; your mother will show up, say something nonsensical while wearing a jellyfish on her head, and then stab you in the heart. And you wake up and think, "Oh, of course, this is about that incident that happened when I was five."

That kind of logically disconnected but emotionally true atmosphere dominates when we're working with the Moon. It doesn't make sense for us to do this, but it feels right, so we're doing it without ever really being sure why.

James Joyce's *Finnegans Wake* was his "night" novel, written heavily under the influence of the Moon. He wanted to write something that felt like a dream, like the workings of the unconscious. He included works of mythology and fables (both of which, according to psychologists such as Sigmund Freud and Carl Jung, work on the unconscious) and broke the standard novel structure (the book ends midsentence, like a man woken middream) to create a work that has to be understood more like a dream than a novel in order to make heads or tails of it.

But the story in *Finnegans Wake* is not the point; it is the poetry of the language, the atmosphere, the dark beauty of the imagery. As it's not written like a standard novel, it cannot be read like one, either. It helps to read it aloud and dip in and out rather than to sit down and read it straight through.

The Moon means you get to throw out all of the rules you've been taught about structure, logic, and meaning and go with your intuition. It's not easy to pull off without becoming too obscure, but the Moon calls us to the task.

RECOMMENDED MATERIALS

The Surrealist Manifestos, booklets by André Breton
The Owl Answers, play by Adrienne Kennedy
Finnegans Wake, book by James Joyce
"Rabbit's Moon," film directed by Kenneth Anger

··— THE SUN – XIX —··

A child stands in the sunlight, arms outstretched. Sometimes he is astride a horse. The child's expression is joyful.

The Sun brings clarity. It also brings warmth, trust, and joy. It can indicate a good relationship, a return to good times, or a sudden realization. It is found at number nineteen.

After the dreaminess of the Moon, we're back in the rational world with the Sun. The lights are all back on, we can see our way ahead clearly, we have a gentle understanding of what our situation is.

The Sun is the *Aha!* moment of Newton's apple and Archimedes's "Eureka!" It is the card of the breakthrough and the intuitive leap. We can struggle and struggle with a problem, feeling like we will never make progress, we will never be able to solve for *X*, and then all of a sudden, bang! We get it.

And that feels good.

The Sun is also just a card of trust. Everything is revealed; there are no secrets or deceptions. You can get a good look at everything that is in front of you. When the Sun appears, there's no need to worry about any hidden motivations or maneuverings. You are able to be forthright and honest, and so are the people with whom you are dealing.

Light has often been a symbol of truth and reason. Superstitions and things that remain unconscious are paired with the dark, because we can't quite see them clearly or understand them. Hence the name of the Enlightenment, where thinkers and philosophers strove to clear the world of superstition and unreason and replace it with clear, rational thought.

It's important to remember that what looks like the sun is not always the Sun. While many of the figures of the Enlightenment did much to advance science and philosophy, many of them thought they were being perfectly logical even when they weren't. Voltaire wrote some shockingly racist tracts, arguing that other races were far inferior to whites, who were the most evolved race. Others found rational justifications for their own misogyny and xenophobia. The rational mind can play tricks, so it is important to, as your algebra teacher would say, check your work. Make sure that the easy insight didn't come because it's wrong, but rather because you are so intelligent.

But for the most part, this is a card of joy and warmth. If you've been going through a difficult, troubling time, this marker tells you that it is over. If your project has been delayed or stalled, if your output has been tortured and slow, this is a sign that you should take the free-and-easy approach. There is something quite playful about this card. The easiness of it allows you to enjoy yourself again rather than struggle, and the act of creation becomes something akin to how you felt about your Lego set when you were a kid.

RECOMMENDED MATERIALS

"Archaic Torso of Apollo," poem by Rainer Maria Rilke

The Proper Study of Mankind: An Anthology of Essays, book by
  Isaiah Berlin

Sunset, painting by Odilon Redon

JUDGMENT – XX

Jesus returns to Earth to judge the living and the dead. The dead rise from their graves, their bodily integrity restored. An angel of the Lord sounds a trumpet in the sky.

While certainly there are religious overtones to the name of the card and its imagery, religious feeling is not necessary to interpret the card. Most religions, from Egyptian to Christian, have had some sort of mechanism for judgment after life, and this merely mimics the idea. It is an accounting of your mistakes and the damage you have done, and a call for you to make amends. Judgment is at number twenty.

How many of the world's artists were terrible people? Oh, so many. The American writer Gertrude Stein was a Vichy France collaborator. French novelist Louis-Ferdinand Céline was a full-on Nazi. Arthur Koestler, the Hungarian-born writer, was a rapist. Legendary jazz trumpeter Miles Davis beat his wives, Michelangelo da Caravaggio, an Italian painter in the late sixteenth and early seventeenth centuries, was a murderer. And on and on.

How many of them were able to fully understand and atone for their mistakes? Hardly any.

I can think of one, though. Romania's Emil Cioran, one of the greatest philosophers of the twentieth century, fell under the sway of the Nazis when they first rose to power. He got a little too swept up by their rhetoric of strength and power; a little too starry-eyed in regard to the control and order they brought to their country. Many intellectuals and thinkers, from Knut Hamsun to Martin Heidegger, fell under the same spell—the exact people who should have known better.

Eventually Cioran was able to see the error in his thinking, and he used that mistake to think through a new round of philosophical thought. He atoned through philosophy. He was one of the few.

That is the feeling of Judgment. The need for absolution. The subject on the card here is the return of Jesus Christ to earth to judge the living and the dead. But to believe in that, we'd need to believe in the concept of sin, and we're beyond that, you and me. Still, the sensation is useful to us: this idea of judging your past wrongs, dealing with the ramifications, and making amends. Probably you don't have Nazi worship in your past, but there are all sorts of other ways we hurt others and go wrong in our thinking.

Judgment is a difficult task, but it offers a karmic restart. In order to progress as people, or through a project, first we must find the moment that progress has stalled. There we will usually find an error. Instead of dealing with our misjudgments and the moments we were at our worst, we often just pile other things on top of them in the hopes they'll go away. That time we betrayed a friend and caused her serious harm? We don't talk about it or think about it; in fact, we don't really even see that friend anymore.

It is a bit like the Alcoholics Anonymous idea of making amends by going through your past, and expressing ruthless honesty and sincere remorse. This card doesn't necessarily have to do with your personal life; it could be a problem with your project that you are refusing to acknowledge and for which you are now just trying to compensate. Maybe you stole a part of someone else's work? Maybe you took credit for something you did not do? Maybe you willfully hurt someone with your portrayal of him or her? Come clean. Make amends.

It might not be a comfortable card, but Judgment does offer a new beginning. A life after death. But it's a card that knows that in order to be reborn, you must die first.

RECOMMENDED MATERIALS

The New Gods, book by Emil Cioran
The Cantos, epic poem by Ezra Pound
Don Giovanni, opera by Wolfgang Amadeus Mozart

THE WORLD.

THE WORLD – XXI

A naked figure, hermaphroditic, stands at the center of a circle of garlands. In her hands are two staffs. She stands before or atop the world. In the corners of the card are the symbols of the four fixed signs of the zodiac: the bull for Taurus, the lion for Leo, the eagle for Scorpio, and the human for Aquarius.

The World is completion. It is feeling at ease in the world, feeling unthreatened and fully accepted as you are. You need for nothing and want for nothing. The fixed signs indicate that things are stable for you, and that you are able to make real changes now if you wish. It is the last card in the Major Arcana, represented by number twenty-one.

This is the end of a long journey. What started with the Fool, with that stepping-off-the-edge-of-the-universe kind of optimism and going through transformation after transformation, now ends with the World. It is wholeness and completion. And it is just the briefest of stops before you have to begin again.

While many of the cards in the deck are about internal processes, the World is as external as it is internal. Most of the other cards are about you. What you need to be learning, what you need to be achieving, what you need to be doing. The World indicates that some of those processes are over. You've completed a project, you've attained a skill, you've accomplished something important. And there is definitely a feeling of self-satisfaction in that.

But the World also means that the outside world—whether that be your field, your community, your family, your peers, or whomever—responds to your achievement. When we're proud of ourselves, we walk around differently. More confidently, more sure of ourselves. And that can change people's responses to us. But the World says: "These other people that you've been trying to impress? They take notice of you." You are able to see real results of the work that you have done.

So it's a card of acceptance. Acceptance of yourself and acceptance by the people around you. You're not, of course, going to win the Pulitzer Prize every time you pull this card, but that is maybe a good way to think about it. It's that sensation of being appreciated and acknowledged.

Now, every card has its darker side, even the World. If we are too focused and too daydreamy about this acceptance, it can be difficult to finish the actual work. We can be so rushed to finish something—just to have it out the door so that we can start a new project—that we don't take the time to bring the project to completion. It just kind of ends. The World calls for refinement and wholeness, not "Oh, it's good enough."

To realize the World, we have to be willing to be a participant in it. That requires some vulnerability. We can secret away our work, stuffing manuscripts in drawers and paintings in attics, because we don't want to risk having someone react negatively to our work or be criticized. And that's a mistake. Not everything we do will be a gem. The World requires vulnerability, which means it requires us to listen to criticism and to suffer disappointment. Because how else will we be able to move people, help people, unless we actively take part in the world?

RECOMMENDED MATERIALS

"The Tortoise and the Hare" in *Aesop's Fables*, book by Aesop
Isaac Bashevis Singer's Nobel Prize acceptance speech

THE ACES

And so we begin.

The Aces are seeds. They can appear as small glimmers, little ideas or notions that, given time, will turn into something unpredictable but magnificent. Or they can appear like an angel from heaven, bestowing a gift upon you. You're just walking around, on your way to the market to buy some eggs, and all of a sudden, wham! You know exactly what you want to do, and the feeling is so intense it is like someone set you on fire.

Those are the Aces. They can either appear to indicate something wholly new, a new book or a new song worming its way into your brain. Or they can show up in the middle of the process, a new approach to clarify and enhance what you are doing.

Aces need to be nurtured. When they show up, it's important to pay attention to the suit and to how they materialize in your life. Document it. Because Aces have the potential to grow and grow, but the only way to make sure that happens is to do the real work.

The downside of the Aces, if there is such a thing, is that they tend to indicate that this new thing is going to take awhile to develop. It's a long road from the Ace to the Ten—the Ten marking a completion of some kind. Aces require courage and patience. They must be embraced and encouraged. They can be disruptive—

anything new generally has to disrupt what you were working on before. But they are pure potential, and as such should be greeted with gratitude.

ACE OF SWORDS

A new idea or philosophy that helps you to find clarity and cut through any tangles.

ACE OF CUPS

A new emotional connection or source of inspiration.

ACE OF WANDS

A kind of holy fire; a new source of passion and excitement.

ACE OF COINS

The seed for something that turns into something real, something tangible that exists in the world.

ACE OF SWORDS

A hand presents a sword from the heavens.

The Ace of Swords is perhaps the only truly positive Swords card. It is a fresh idea, a new start, or an intellectual breakthrough. It can also be a moment of truth. Something verbal or mental that startles and resets.

William James was having a difficult time. The twenty-eight-year-old had started several different projects—several different career paths, actually: painting, medical school, adventuring in Brazil—and nothing seemed right to him. He was feeling like a failure, trying to find his way out of his depression, but he was beginning to believe that he was incapable of making decisions and real changes in his life.

Then, on April 30, 1870, he recorded in his journal a kind of epiphany: "My first act of free will shall be to believe in free will." If James wanted to decide on a course of action, his first decision was going to be that he could decide on a course of action. It was a kind of loopy logic, but one that helped him out of his funk and became a kind of centerpiece to the philosophical system he helped to establish: pragmatism—the belief that whether an idea or an action is the right one depends on whether the end result is a practical success.

That is an Ace of Swords moment: one idea, one philosophy, one thought that cuts through the haze and acts as a kind of guiding light. Once you have that idea, it feels like Excalibur. You can wield it to get results, and it gives you a kind of unlimited power to face down uncertainty.

What you do with that idea is, of course, up to you. You can develop it into a scientific theory. You can shape it into a book. You can use it as a kind of philosophical backbone to any creative endeavor you pursue. The Ace of Swords is strong enough to take on any form you wish.

Use it as a beacon to guide you forward.

RECOMMENDED MATERIALS

Pragmatism, book of lectures by William James
The Principia, book by Isaac Newton
View from the Window at Le Gras, photograph (world's oldest surviving photo) by Joseph Nicéphore Niépce

ACE OF CUPS

A cup, overflowing. Often with a dove of hope descending from the heavens.

This is a peak emotional experience. Frequently equated with love, but it can also be joy, contentment, gratitude. Anything that overwhelms. This card also represents the soul, in the context of religious or spiritual experiences.

The traditional reading of the Ace of Cups, outside of a creative framework, is falling in love. It's a sensation that can either feel like being hit by a bus or some gentle, gradual understanding that takes over your entire existence.

Within our creative context, though, that feeling of falling in love can take on many forms. There can be an overwhelming sense of emotional connection to a work that is deeply important to you. Or the Ace of Cups can show up as the beginning of a project about love and connection. It can also be a strong sense of inspiration: a painting, a book, or a movie that moves you to create a response to it. Or it can introduce you to a muse. But it's important to remember that the Cups rule the soul.

For the mystics, the love of God has been as important as the love of a person, and through the centuries, their work—usually a little loony, usually a little out of step with whatever anyone else is doing—has documented the power of that love. There was W. B. Yeats, contacting the spirit world for his poetry; eleventh-century nun St. Hildegard of Bingen creating beautiful drawings and musical compositions while communicating directly with God; the American poet James Merrill hunched over a Ouija board and transcribing the results.

But perhaps the greatest of these spiritual compositions was Johann Sebastian Bach's plan to compose chorale cantatas for services for the entire liturgical year. Bach was a devout Lutheran, and so he focused much of his attention on creating sacred music. The cantatas were intended for church services, and the results are haunting. Meant to elevate the spirit of the listener, they are eerie in their otherworldliness. Bach not only translated his own love for God beautifully but also created something that would have an almost physical impact on audiences.

One does not have to be religious to embrace the Ace of Cups. Love takes all kinds of forms, but here it is its overwhelming quality that matters. The way it can turn you into a better person; bring you to a higher version of yourself.

Find your inspiration and fall in love with it. Write to it, sing to it, pay it tribute in images and in words. It can be a well for you that is unlikely to run dry.

RECOMMENDED MATERIALS

Chorale cantatas, composed by J. S. Bach
The Changing Light of Sandover, epic poem by James Merrill
Illuminations of Hildegard of Bingen, book by Matthew Fox

-•- ACE OF WANDS -•-

A wand, presented from the heavens, made out of wood, often sprouting new green leaves.

The Ace of Wands sparks courage and inspiration. It readies you for a new adventure. It can also represent sexual feelings; an overwhelming desire. With the Ace of Wands, you find faith—in yourself, with the divine, with another. It is often experienced as intense excitement.

The Ace of Wands is the most ephemeral of all of the Aces. One can easily become overcome with passion, anger, excitement, but it is very difficult to sustain. If you become distracted for a minute, the sensation passes, and you forget what you were on about.

At the same time, it can also be the most overwhelming of the Aces. It is the feeling of being taken to another plane of existence, almost. It can be the feeling of possession, that something—an idea or perhaps another being—has descended upon you. The question then becomes how to work with that. It's hard to get a lot of work done when your hair is on fire.

We should ask St. Teresa of Avila. She experienced holy visions, visitations by God that shook her both in body and in spirit. There is a famous sculpture by the seventeenth-century Italian artist Bernini that shows St. Teresa awash in a state of ecstasy from her communion with God. She described these visitations as painful, "yet so surpassing was the sweetness of this excessive pain, that I could not wish to be rid of it."

These feelings became the basis of her great collection of writing, as she tried to explain the connection between one person and the Other. The Other can be God, or a lover, or any other kind of intimate. Her writings are a philosophy of passion: how it causes us to lose ourselves, but also how we find ourselves—maybe our best selves—in that state.

The Ace of Wands is an experience that must then be translated into some other form, whether it be philosophy, like St. Teresa, or dance, or whatever else you choose. The difficulty of this card is its resistance to being pinned down. You might have to look to the other cards that you've pulled in a reading to help guide you into working with the Ace of Wands.

RECOMMENDED MATERIALS

The Interior Castle, book by St. Teresa of Avila
The Ecstasy of Saint Teresa, sculpture by Bernini
"The Judgment," short story by Franz Kafka

⊷ ACE OF COINS ⊷

A coin, presented in a hand, set above a fecund garden.

The Ace of Coins indicates fertility, both literal and metaphorical. It is a new sense of security, found through work and determination. It is more realistic than the other Aces, something that will lead to prosperity in one form or another.

Think of the Ace of Coins as an anchor. Think of it as the pen hitting paper, the brush stroking canvas. There might have been ideas swirling around, diffuse and dissipating, but now it is time to actually start the work.

Coins rule matter and the real world, and so this card is about starting to put form to the inspiration. Of all the Aces, this is the least obvious. The other three, Swords, Cups, and Wands, can knock you upside the head and take over your entire life. The

Coins card is subtle, because it is the beginning of making something. And one can work only so quickly. It is the chisel going into the marble, something that takes time and delicacy, rather than the inspiration for the finished product, which can appear all at once out of nowhere.

The Ace of Coins also brings stability. It turns dreams and ideas into reality, and that can be a very grounding process for some. The painter Yayoi Kusama had a mind that played tricks on her. She suffered from hallucinations at times: the pattern on the tablecloth would expand until it was crawling over the walls, the floor, up her legs. But the act of creating something from those visions rooted her and brought her back to reality. If she re-created on canvas the patterns she saw, the visions could be brought under control. They could be worked with instead of against.

Which is not to say that you need to go mad to get the most out of the Ace of Coins. But it can be a stabilizing force, to take the potential, this idea—maybe from one of the other Aces—that leaves you trembling and overly excited, and make something out of it.

The Ace of Coins means that you should assess your discipline and work process as well. If you're waiting for divine inspiration, you might be waiting forever. Start the work and see what happens.

RECOMMENDED MATERIALS

Ascension of Polka Dots on the Trees, environmental art by
　　Yayoi Kusama

The Eames chair and ottoman, furniture designed by
　　Charles and Bernice "Ray" Eames

Schema, sculpture by Eva Hesse

"Marie-Louise," recording by Wendo Kolosoy

THE TWOS

The Twos are, naturally, all about balance. You had one thing; now you have another. It's up to you to figure out how to fit them together, choose between them, or strike a balance between them. It can often be like a juggling act, trying to hold two separate ideas or realities at the same time.

And where there is balance, there is imbalance. Think about your own life. Do you find yourself sacrificing one thing for something else? Your free time for a promotion at work? Your creative work for your children? Wherever you feel pulled apart by two contradictory demands, that is where a Two will show up.

If you work it right, however, the Twos don't have to be in conflict. Rather than pulling you apart, a Two card can show you how two different influences or demands can be brought together to form something completely new. Instead of a choice between red or blue, you'll find that the answer is actually "purple."

Until you figure out how to do that, the Twos can feel a little chaotic. Don't fret; it's a minor problem. No one here is having a really bad time. It's just a matter of reprioritizing, rethinking, restrategizing. Things are easily put to rest.

TWO OF SWORDS

This is what looks like a yes-or-no decision, or maybe a pros-and-cons list. It's a stubborn problem, though, one that can lead to indecision.

TWO OF CUPS

This requires a balance between two people: either your partner or perhaps a collaborator.

TWO OF WANDS

This is the point between what you have and what there is potential for; what is settled and what is still possible.

TWO OF COINS

Upheaval, a sense of imbalance. This can either feel disturbing or like a lot of fun. It really depends on how you respond to the changes.

·•· TWO OF SWORDS ·•·

A woman sits with her back to the sea. She crosses two large swords in front of her to form an X at her neck. She is often shown blind-folded.

Frequently described as representing "indecision," the Two of Swords requires simply that a decision be made. The two swords appear equal in every respect: weight, appearance, sharpness. This is what leads to her inability to decide. Note that the swords seem to cut her in two, her head from her body. That and her refusal to look at the sea behind her both suggest that she has cut herself off from her intuition, and that is where the decision actually lies.

You can do this, or you can do that. The problem is that the choices will lead you down incredibly different paths, and yet they look equally tempting somehow. As a result, you have reached a kind of stasis of indecision. When two possibilities look the same and yet so very different, how can you ever make a decision?

Not with a pros-and-cons list. Oftentimes we reach this point of indecision because we are trying to make a decision logically rather than intuitively. We are working from what we think that we want rather than what we actually want. So adding up the potential virtues and downsides of each option will only lead us further into stagnation instead of providing some perspective. After all, how does one weigh every pro and every con? How does one calculate potential joy or potential despair?

A client of mine was accepted into two different art schools. One was on the East Coast; the other was in the Southwest. One was prestigious, the other was radical. At one school, she knew people who were familiar with her work. At the other, she knew no one, and so she could completely reinvent herself there.

This, of course, became a decision not just about where she wanted to spend the next few years. It became a crisis of "What kind of life do I want?" She was giving each option so much meaning—the ability to change her entire life—that she couldn't even begin to figure out how to decide between them. Obviously a choice like this *would* change her life, but she had forgotten about free will: the ability to change her mind. She forgot she was a fully formed human and not just a lump of clay to be shaped by someone else's will.

Relax. Go with your gut. Stop giving each option so much power. The important thing is simply to make a decision. Your ability to choose gives the situation meaning, not the situation itself.

RECOMMENDED MATERIALS

"The Road Not Taken," poem by Robert Frost

On Balance, book by Adam Phillips

Broadcast News, film directed by James L. Brooks

·◦· TWO OF CUPS ·◦·

A man and a woman stand together, each holding a cup. In some versions of the card, above the union of the two cups hangs a caduceus, or two entwined snakes with wings at the top.

Both cups are of equal size and apparent value, which indicates a relationship of equals; a relationship in perfect balance. No one has power over the other. The caduceus is a symbol of healing, showing that the relationship—which does not have to be romantic but can indicate friendship or a business partnership—brings goodness to each party.

With the Two of Cups, it's not just another circumstance or idea that you have to work into a balance, it's a whole other person. A person with his or her own needs, desires, and ideas. The act of collaboration can be inspiring, or it can drive people insane.

Rather than the muse dynamic, where one person is doing all of the work and the other person just has to exist, here each person has to see the other as an equal. The Two of Cups is traditionally a marriage card; a wholly egalitarian relationship. When we put it into the artistic context, it becomes a collaboration where each partner feels that his or her ideas are being heard, and each person gets equal credit. Certainly throughout time there have been men who have taken credit for their wives' work, like the painter Walter Keane, who claimed that he'd painted his wife Margaret's paintings of big-eyed children, which were a runaway success in the 1950s and '60s. But with the Two of Cups, mutual respect is required.

Collaboration has led to important work, such as the Wright Brothers' experiments in flight, or Dutch fashion designers Viktor Horsting and Rolf Snoeren cocreating the successful and influential fashion house Viktor & Rolf. The performance artists Marina Abramović and Ulay were lovers as well as collaborators, and much of their work together explored what it is like for two people to become a single unit. Their androgynous and unified work, like their performance *Relation in Time*—where they sat back-to-back for seventeen hours, their long hair knotted together—expressed this idea of equality to the point where it was sometimes difficult to tell the two apart.

The Two of Cups does not need to imply romance. There have certainly been many actor-and-director film collaborations that embody the Two of Cups dynamic, such as Michael Fassbender's three films with director Steve McQueen, and Catherine Keener's work with director Nicole Holofcener.

But it does require respect, mutual admiration, and a level playing field. The Two of Cups asks you to take on another person and to allow him or her to work with you rather than for you.

RECOMMENDED MATERIALS

Rest Energy, short film (part of a series) by Marina Abramović and
 Ulay
My Life in the Bush of Ghosts, recording by Brian Eno and
 David Byrne
Hunger, film directed by Steve McQueen
Radioactive: Marie & Pierre Curie, book by Lauren Redniss

--◆-- TWO OF WANDS --◆--

A man stands holding a tall wand in his hand. The second wand is planted in the ground behind him. He looks off into the distance, holding in his other hand an orb, although sometimes this is a globe.

The Two of Wands represents mastery and connection. The man on the card is in control of his situation. What he has is stable, and so now he is looking to expand his horizons. The globe shows a command over the world and a sense of connectedness.

This is a great card to pull for a creative project because it suggests that you are now in a position of power. You are good at what you do, and you've progressed in your abilities and in your confidence so that now you can take time to assess where you have come from and where you still want to go.

The Two of Wands requires a sense of scope. To remain in a

position of control, you need to strike a balance between intake and output, between expansion and maintaining what you already have. It is also a good time to think about the past: Was there something you wanted to do at some point, but you didn't have the skills or the energy or the time? Now that you have these things, and this card suggests you do, it might be time to take on that task.

Be like the female pharaoh Hatshepsut. During her reign, from 1479 to 1458 BC, Egypt flourished. She strengthened the infrastructure while also establishing new trade routes that brought wealth and new allies. She used diplomacy against her rivals but was also willing to go into battle.

It's the same feeling of tending to the old but also bringing in the new. Now that you're in a position of strength, what are you going to do with it? Talk to your peers, establish your own little spice trade. Find new sources of inspiration and inspire others with your work. Push yourself to dream bigger and strategize how to make those dreams reality.

This is a card that feels really good. Use it well.

RECOMMENDED MATERIALS

Journeys on the Silk Road, book by Joyce Morgan and
   Conrad Walters
Seated Statue of Hatshepsut (artist unknown)
The Woman Who Would Be King, book by Kara Cooney

·•· TWO OF COINS ·•·

A man balances two large coins in his hands. Behind him is the sea, with a ship or two setting off on a journey. The man is either dancing or perhaps falling; he is not quite balanced. Likewise, the Coins are not balanced. A figure eight, the mathematical symbol for infinity, encircles the two Coins.

The imbalance of the Coins and the man shows that things here are unstable. And yet the look on his face is happy. It is an imbalance that is bringing him pleasure rather than pain. Something new has arrived, it has to be incorporated with the old, and that means things have to be shifted. The Two of Coins represents that shift. Also, this card has been associated traditionally with the beginning of travel.

It's time to take on a new task. A new project that complements what you're already doing but is also a diversion. Sometimes we decide we need to hunker down and focus, to pour all of our energy and time into one thing. But then when we actually sit down to do the focusing and the pouring, we stare blankly at the empty page or the blank canvas. Sometimes juggling two things at once allows you to give more to each because one project inspires the other.

Many painters set up multiple canvases in their studio. If they're not feeling inspired to work on one, maybe the other one needs some attention. It helps them stay productive and also keeps the situation light. They don't feel blocked because there's not that stress of "This one painting is everything right now."

In 1917, Virginia Woolf and her husband, Leonard, set up Hogarth Press, a small publisher that printed beautiful little books by hand. They published their peers and their friends. The couple ran the company at the same time that Virginia was writing her most important works, and in fact, both she and Hogarth Press enjoyed their most productive periods at the same time.

Each project, the publishing and the writing, gave her an outlet for the other. Neither was allowed to become too oppressive, because when one no longer flowed easily, she could just move on to the other. It kept her stimulated and engaged; there was less time to stare at the wall, feeling frustrated and blocked. It refocused her energy.

Sometimes when we're feeling overwhelmed, we think we need to remove outside obligations. But it's often those outside obligations that keep us sane. We can actually improve productivity by adding to our to-do list.

RECOMMENDED MATERIALS

Mrs. Dalloway, book by Virginia Woolf

Kora in Hell: Improvisations, book by William Carlos Williams

Photographs of Claude Monet's studio, available online

THE THREES

After the wobbliness of the Twos, we get our first sense of stability with the Threes. If you want to build something, bring more of something into your life, then you need a solid foundation. The Threes are the first cards that allow for that, and they show you how to start to build *up* instead of just *out*.

Because of that, we get our first sense of the scope of our projects with the Threes. There is a pivot from daydreaming or noodling around with the idea and really putting it into perspective. It's time to take stock of how long this might take, what materials you will need, what skills you are going to need to hone to do the best job here.

In order to build a solid foundation, one has to know what is going to go up on top. Think of it like architecture. You have to know how tall you want to build before you can know how far deep down you have to excavate. Your preparation here is important, and the work you do with the Threes will either pay off in the long run, or you'll realize midway through that you should have taken this part of it more seriously.

A Three drawn at the beginning of a project is going to function differently than a Three drawn midway through the process. If you're just starting out, think seriously about where you plan on taking this. Look out at the horizon and prepare for what you're going to need once you start moving toward it. If you are already halfway there, the suit will tell you where you might have deficiencies. Pull the Three of Wands? Maybe you didn't bring in enough passion at the beginning. You'll need to turn your attention to the beginning stages and see if you overlooked something. It's not too late to do some foundation repair.

THREE OF SWORDS

The darkest of the Threes, this card says that you have accumulated suffering around the foundation of an old wound. This calls for an uprooting.

THREE OF CUPS

This card is about community and companionship. There's an emotional stability here, brought on by a circle of supportive friends.

THREE OF WANDS

Here you are asked to cultivate a sense of adventure. It's about creating a life of passion, about approaching new opportunities with excitement instead of fear.

THREE OF COINS

The work here is for something lasting and permanent—a building named after you or perhaps a cathedral.

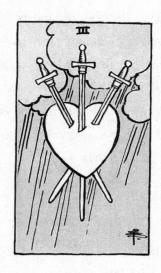

⚊•⚬• THREE OF SWORDS •⚬•⚊

A heart, pierced by three swords, is set against a stormy backdrop.

The most important thing to note is the lack of gore in this card. A heart is pierced by swords, and yet there is no gushing of blood. That suggests the swords have been there for a long time. The injury is an old one. Also note the lack of a human figure on the card (in most versions). It's almost an impersonal pain, something that has been there so long it's all but become abstract to the person who is suffering.

It is a cliché, Lord knows, but Ovid's advice "Be patient and tough. One day this pain will be useful to you" is still true for artists.

We all experience betrayal, abandonment, cruelty, and pain. The question is what happens after that. Do we flinch every time someone raises his hand to us? Do we try to attain some understanding of how the wound came to be and a sense of empathy for the person who hurt us? Do we use it as a source of strength or as an excuse to be weak?

Old hurts—those inflicted by our families or during childhood—hold a kind of influence over us our entire lives. We find ourselves stuck in patterns that we don't always understand. But as artists, it is important to expose that old wound and understand its influence.

Think of the Charlotte Brontë novel *Jane Eyre*. Jane's actions with her suitors Rochester and St. John make sense only because of what Charlotte wrote about Jane's childhood of abuse and neglect. It is her fear of never being chosen and never feeling love that drives her decisions. If that history of abandonment had been glossed over to get to the action of the romance later on in the book, Jane would have looked simply foolish or stubborn. Instead, she feels perfectly human, and her feelings, thoughts, and deeds, holistically understandable.

It takes an intense understanding of human nature and psychology to convey a coherent sense of a person's motivations. And what better way to reach that understanding than to examine your own cause and effect, and those of the people you love? It takes love and patience to deal properly with the Three of Swords. And yet work that is based on this particular foundation and all of the intricate ways it drives our impulses—work based on deep, old hurts—resonates deeply with audiences.

RECOMMENDED MATERIALS

Jane Eyre, book by Charlotte Brontë
In Memoriam A. H. H., epic poem by Alfred Lord Tennyson
The Glass Essay, epic poem by Anne Carson

·•· THREE OF CUPS ·•·

Three women dancing together in a field lift their cups to one another.

There are two meanings to this card. The one reflected by the imagery is that of female companionship. The women are friends and are enjoying one another's company. The other meaning comes from simply the type of card: three cups equals three hearts. It can represent a triangulated relationship.

A creative spirit needs companionship. With this particular card, that companionship is not about having someone edit or review your work to tell you whether or not you are on the right track. It's about needing friends to keep you company, to inspire you, to bring you a kind of buoyancy. It's the go-out-and-get-drunk-with-your-girlfriends card.

The Three of Cups is specifically about female friendship. That does not mean the card isn't relevant to you men out there reading this. Men should have women friends, too. There is a lightness, an empathy, and a strong connection between lifelong female friends. They pick you up when you're down, they will talk you through your problems, they will bring you champagne when you have something worth celebrating. (If your friends are good enough, they will look at just about everything you do as worthy of celebrating with champagne.)

Certainly the friendship between the political philosopher Hannah Arendt and the novelist and critic Mary McCarthy was something worth envying. In their letters, compiled in the 1995 book *Between Friends*, you can see them working through their ideas, but also commiserating and offering support when one of them received a bad review or didn't get something she wanted. Sometimes, though, they just talked about boys. Even if you are one of the most brilliant writers of the twentieth century, you need to talk about boys now and then! That doesn't make you any less of a genius, it simply means you are human.

Reading through the letters, you're inspired by how women encourage and support each other. Female friendships are so often portrayed as catty or sabotaging, when they are in truth incredibly complex. Having a close circle of friends to offer love and support can see you through just about any difficulty and setback. It can also be a healthy source of inspiration. But it also shows you how to portray a love that is not romantic.

RECOMMENDED MATERIALS

Between Friends: The Correspondence of Hannah Arendt and Mary McCarthy, 1949–1975, book edited by Carol Brightman

The Mitfords: Letters Between Six Sisters, book edited by Charlotte Mosley

The Women, film directed by George Cukor

⋅⊷⋅ THREE OF WANDS ⋅⊶⋅

A man stands at the edge of a cliff. He holds one wand in his hand, the other two are planted behind him. He stares off toward the horizon, over the sea, at the ships on the water.

This is a card of travel and transition. The man is about to set off on a journey of some kind, as indicated by the ship. But it is also worth noticing that the man is changing modes of travel. He has walked to the edge of the earth, now he is at the sea and must change from foot to boat. So a change is coming that is going to require some adaptation.

How does one go about building a foundation for a life that is filled with passion and adventure? The story of Richard Francis Burton is perhaps the best place to start for inspiration.

Passion can be fleeting. Once it meets reality, it can dissipate easily. You wanted an adventure, but once you actually got out into the desert and got sand in your underwear, your skin started to blister, and you wandered off the trail and couldn't find your way back, you decided what you really wanted was indoor plumbing and your own bed.

So how to sustain it? For Burton—a nineteenth-century explorer who was the first to summit several mountains, sought the source of the Nile River, and was the first Westerner to sneak into Mecca and describe what he saw—he was able to keep up the excitement through all of the groundwork he put into his preparations. He spoke dozens of languages and dialects, learned through intense study. He was employed as a counsel by the British government, which sent him on missions throughout the world. He collaborated with other explorers and used the writing he did during and after his travels to guide his itineraries.

It's not as spontaneous as buying an international airline ticket on a whim and heading off with no real idea of what you will do once you arrive, but novelty wears thin after awhile. And Burton, who was able to converse with the locals, write extensively about the nations he visited, and bring back volumes of literature and translate them into English for the first time—we have him to thank for the *Kama Sutra*—got more out of his experiences that way.

But one cannot always be off on an adventure and expect to get any real work done. If you are always off chasing that glimmering thing on the horizon, you'll never find the focus needed to see a project through from beginning to end. Even Burton himself didn't complete his greatest works until he settled down in a house with a wife and furniture and kitchen cabinets. If the Three of Wands seems familiar to you, you might want to make sure it's not your default setting to run away every time responsibility comes calling. Sometimes settling down, turning away from your ever-present curiosity, is the brave thing to do.

RECOMMENDED MATERIALS

A Rage to Live: A Biography of Richard and Isabel Burton, book by
    Mary S. Lovell
Tracks, film directed by John Curran
Dust in the Lion's Paw, book by Freya Stark

·-· THREE OF COINS ·-·

Three figures are constructing a building together, each charged with a different task.

This is the beginning of a large project, one that will require outside help and will probably call for several different skill sets to complete.

Consider this card to be the building of a cathedral. It is going to be a long, arduous project. It is going to take a wide variety of skills: masonry, woodworking, stained glass design. You probably are not going to be able to do this on your own; you will need assistance from others. And the end result will be magnificent.

There is a sense that a project that begins with the Three of Coins will need to be thoroughly thought out in advance. The foundations have to be strong, and one has to have a sense of what the final product will be before you begin. Otherwise you'll be three-quarters of the way through and find that your buttresses don't line up with your naves. (Not sure if this is a problem someone would actually have—I'm not really so great on cathedral design.)

Best, then, to think of it as a serious construction project. Start with the blueprints, and begin sketching out how you envision the project when it is finished. Take the measurements, and decide which supplies you'll need throughout. Find the best possible collaborators. Not people whose company you enjoy—although that is important, too—but people whose strengths compensate for your weaknesses and people who can do the things you are not good at. Lay the foundation and then work slowly but steadily.

The other thing to consider about cathedrals is what goes on inside. It is the container for something divine, or at the very least, something bigger than yourself. It's not only about you—the ego has to get out of the way with this card in many different ways. Both to work with others but also to allow the audience to dwell within the project. You might want to take that into consideration when you are in the planning stages, and allow people to use your work in ways that perhaps you would not.

The power of this card is in its potential. It is the beginning of something big. If you pull this card midproject, though, you might have to revisit your plans and make sure they are still serving you.

RECOMMENDED MATERIALS

Fallingwater, house designed by Frank Lloyd Wright
Siena Cathedral
Bauhaus Women: Art, Handicraft, Design, book by Ulrike Müller

THE FOURS

Fours are all about order. They help us see how to structure our projects, but also whether all of that order or discipline might be choking the life out of what we are doing.

Some creatives work better with a framework in place before beginning their work, while others work more intuitively. What works for one person is going to inhibit another. One person might need set hours in which to work because a strict schedule helps him or her focus. Others might find this to be intimidating and prefer to stay flexible.

Pulling a Four card indicates that you need to rethink not only the backbone of your work but also the way in which you organize your work process. Routine can be helpful, but it can also kill spontaneity. In a similar way, a solid structure to your project—working from an outline, say—can either help or hinder your progress. It's important to remember that each project might require a different structure and a different sort of discipline. Some works are as floppy as a jellyfish, and others as tightly controlled as exoskeletons.

So no matter which Four you draw, and no matter how you choose to organize your work and your process, there is a sense here that you need to bring some order to the chaos. If you are having a difficult time maintaining focus or seeing a way to the end of the project, a Four will provide a little guidance.

FOUR OF SWORDS

Here the stability means that you get to take a nap. Things are solid and okay for now, so you should rest and gain a little perspective, because things are guaranteed to get crazy again.

FOUR OF CUPS

You are so concerned with maintaining order that you are willfully ignoring a new source of inspiration.

FOUR OF WANDS

Creating a sound creative structure, one that allows for deviation and experimentation. Being open and yet still disciplined.

FOUR OF COINS

This card is the strictest of all the Fours; it is all right angles and straight lines. It makes for a strong foundation, but taken too far, it can also be overly limiting.

✦ FOUR OF SWORDS ✦

A knight, often shown still in his armor, rests. Three swords are mounted on his wall, but a fourth sword lies next to his bed.

This is a pause in the battle. The fighter, however, remains vigilant, with his sword by his bed, just in case he is called to duty. The three mounted swords suggest that the battle has been long, but now he must prepare himself and rest so that he does not become exhausted.

This is the card that gives you permission to stay in bed and binge-watch *The Good Wife*. Or maybe you prefer *The Wire*? Either way, this card says you need to take it easy, get some rest, turn off your brain for a while.

It is no good running yourself ragged for the sake of the work. It's one thing to be inspired and engaged and excited to get to work in the morning. It's quite another to sacrifice your sleep and your health and the love of the people around you by staying up all night and not knowing when to quit.

We have this myth of the creator as a superhuman beast: that in order to be a *real* writer or artist, you must push past your limits, you must drive everyone around you crazy, you must work so hard that you end up in a mental institution or dead from a heart attack before you turn fifty. Watch any not-very-good biopic, such as *Pollock*, starring Ed Harris as the tormented abstract expressionist painter, or *The Agony and the Ecstasy*, about the battle of wills between Michelangelo and Pope Julius II, who'd commissioned him to paint the ceiling of the Sistine Chapel. You'll see a consumed artist driving himself mad with his intense dedication.

It's nonsense. No one has to work like that.

The Four of Swords advises you to keep things stable enough so that you're not running yourself into the ground. It's easy to mythologize musician Kurt Cobain or the poet Arthur Rimbaud, who drove themselves to extremes for their art and burned out and died or retired young as a result. Harder than that is to be someone who maintains sanity while producing genius work and who is able to keep working consistently over a long career.

Part of that is knowing when *not* to work. There is a time for output but also time for rest, for intake, for seeing what else the world has to offer. And, yes, for self-indulgent times of eating junk food on the couch and watching stupid television.

You have to think of the long-term here, either until the end of the project or until the end of your life. Conserve your resources accordingly.

RECOMMENDED MATERIALS

Lives of Girls and Women, book by Alice Munro

"Take Breaks," recording by the Brutal Knights

"Bartleby, the Scrivener: A Story of Wall Street," short story by
Herman Melville

⋅⋆⋅ FOUR OF CUPS ⋅⋆⋅

A man or a woman, often shown as a shepherd, sits cross-legged on the ground. His arms are crossed, too, and he looks down at three cups at his feet. A fourth cup, being presented out of the sky, hangs above his head. He is ignoring it, or he does not see it.

The three cups on the ground represent what is real and what exists now. The fourth cup, being gifted to him from the heavens, is the potential. But notice the figure's crossed arms and bowed head. He is purposely closing himself off from this potential. His attention remains with what already exists, rather than with what could be. To look up would require hope, and it would require change. The Four of Cups indicates that you should look up, open yourself up to vulnerability, and imagine a better future.

Here, an idea or a new inspiration is trying to make itself known to you, but you are trying desperately not to notice. There are basically angelic choruses singing above your head, and you have clamped your hands over your ears and are doing your best "La-la-la-la-la, I can't hear you!"

The question is, Why would someone ever ignore something like that? Surely that is what all creatives sit around waiting for: inspiration to strike. But it's disruptive. You might be almost finished with the project, or maybe you have a very clear sense of how you want things to go, and then here comes the big blinking sign that says, "Nope, dummy, this is the way it should be instead!" It means you are going to have to tear apart the work you've already done or maybe abandon it completely to follow this new idea, and who wants to do that?

A client of mine, after spending four years on a manuscript and finishing a complete draft, told me that she suddenly realized during her revisions that the novel should have been written in the first person rather than in the third. She had become so stuck on the idea of a third-person narration that she had ignored the signs this was the wrong approach and plowed through to the end. Now that she was done, she was completely unwilling to fix what she knew to be a very obvious problem.

My client would not have had to start over from the beginning, but certainly admitting that this was the solution to her book's problems would mean another year's worth of work ahead of her. She was so anxious to be done with this book and move on to something else that she was willing to sacrifice the whole thing. Eventually, though, she resigned herself to her task and began the hard work of revision. It took her a long time, but the end result was much improved.

In that way, we can all be like Penelope in Homer's *The Odyssey*, who prayed for her husband Odysseus's return from the protracted Trojan War only to fail to recognize him when he finally showed up. If what we get doesn't fall in line with what we expect, or if what we get is too disruptive, we can fail to see its value. And so we reject it or send it away. Like, "No, I see myself only playing stringed instruments; I have no use for the clarinet." But maybe the clarinet will open up whole new worlds for you if you are willing to give it a try.

With the Four of Cups, you have to maintain an openness and a willingness to be derailed. It's not good to stay stubborn just so that you can stay on schedule or stick with your original vision when a better way is calling out to you.

RECOMMENDED MATERIALS

The Beast in the Jungle, book by Henry James
"The Stranger with the Face of a Man I Loved," recording by
    Sarah Kirkland Snider
Cheerful Weather for the Wedding, book by Julia Strachey

⊰· FOUR OF WANDS ·⊱

Four wands, planted in the ground to form a square, are strung with ribbons and garlands to form a canopy. Behind them, a group of people celebrate with music and dancing.

The Four of Wands is an exciting kind of stability. Instead of four walls closed in and blocking out all light and air, there is almost only light and air. As such, it can be an inadequate shelter, but it is flexible, beautiful, and exciting. This is a card about remaining flexible and not too rooted to the earth. You're allowing for major changes without too much fuss, staying mobile and spontaneous, but you can still rely on a certain amount of stability and support.

The Four of Wands is not only about the work itself, but also about the environment in which you work. Whether you work in a studio or from home, your surroundings have an effect on you. The Four of Wands indicates that you need to find a new space, or at the very least make some changes so that your workspace becomes more stimulating and more supportive.

So often we are at the mercy of our surroundings: the honking traffic that takes us out of our head space, the crying children, the bleak view from a window that overlooks a brick wall or an overflowing garbage can. However, sometimes we're at fault, interrupting a productive period of concentration to "just see if that email came in," only to find ourselves two hours later in the middle of some online game we hate. We spend a lot of time trying to maintain focus with music or earplugs, or setting up programs to disable our internet connection.

The Four of Wands is the ideal: a place that is orderly but is still inspiring. It implies a need for beauty as well as a need for community. This can be as drastic as packing up all of your things and moving to a new city. Certainly places like Paris between the wars and New York in the 1940s and 1950s beckoned artists not only with their cheap rents but also with the idea that you could go there to meet all kinds of like-minded folks and rub elbows with the greatest artists of their time.

Which doesn't necessarily mean you have to get rid of all of your belongings and move to Berlin. It merely indicates that you need to look at where you are physically when you work. Are you getting enough social stimulation? Does your office need to be spruced up with artwork and fresh flowers? Does the city make you feel penned in, and would you work better in the countryside?

Many writers and artists pull inspiration from their surroundings: think of the British author Daphne du Maurier, who wrote novel after novel with the region of Cornwall as her muse. For other examples, look to the so-called Lost Generation in Paris and the Chicago of street photographer Vivian Maier's images. Ask yourself how your own location can become your muse, whether it be your house, your city, or your circle of companions.

RECOMMENDED MATERIALS
Rebecca, book by Daphne du Maurier
Tempe a Paille, house designed by Eileen Gray
Paris Between the Wars, 1919–1939: Art, Life & Culture, book by
  Gérard Durozoi

·–· FOUR OF COINS ·–·

A man or woman sits, clutching to his or her body four coins: two under the feet, one held tightly to the chest, and the other behind the head. Often there is a walled city behind the person.

The Four of Coins is security. But security is often won by shutting out freedom, and that is the trade-off that this card asks you to consider. The figure can appear to be a little paranoid, clinging to all of his possessions in fear that they will be taken away. But it can also be interpreted as having a sense of order and control over one's belongings.

How you respond to the Four of Coins card depends a great deal on how you work and what your personality is like. It's a card that can make one person smile and the next person groan.

If you are a person who needs structure and limitations—some sort of outside stress—in order to do your best work, you'll see the Four of Coins as a positive card. When Eleanor Catton began work on her Man Booker Prize–winning novel *The Luminaries*, she immediately went about putting very tight restrictions on her work. By setting her novel in a specific time and place, and creating an astrological chart for each character, her freedom to do whatever she liked with these men and women was suddenly very restricted: the characters could behave only in the way that their natal charts, and the movements of the planets at that time, allowed.

The Four of Coins is a tight fit. Its rigidity means there is not a lot of room to maneuver; you have to stay within the lines. For Catton, paradoxically, she found the limitations freeing. The internal logic of the work was planned out in advance thanks to the planetary transits of the novel's time; she just had to elaborate on the details.

Many other writers have worked within similarly strict frameworks, like James Joyce fleshing out *Ulysses* on top of *The Odyssey's* bones—Joyce's book uses the structure of *The Odyssey* to plot out the journey of his own characters, so that every action corresponds to a moment in the original epic poem. By knowing the limitations, the writer can know what doesn't belong in the story, which is sometimes just as helpful as knowing what does.

If you are a more intuitive creator, however, the Four of Coins can feel oppressive. Some would rather die than work from an outline, and picking a card that says "You need to hem things in a bit" would be as panic-inducing as a letter from the IRS.

But with the Four of Coins, you need to ask yourself if you're being too restrictive; if your project is configured too tightly. Because if you are relying too heavily on structure, if you're sacrificing style or spontaneity, it can feel as stale as a room with the windows and doors all shut tightly.

RECOMMENDED MATERIALS

The Luminaries, book by Eleanor Catton
The Dream Songs, book of poetry by John Berryman
Anthropology: 101 True Love Stories, book by Dan Rhodes

THE FIVES

Picture the Fives as a wall. Instead of choosing to scale that wall using a ladder or maybe some rope, you've decided you can just batter it down with your head. That is the sensation of the Fives— of the obstacle and the not-so-great plan to move it.

Fives tend to show up in creative projects when you're blocked. You're either doing the same thing over and over again, hoping for different results, or there is an outside force saying, "No, this isn't good enough. Try again." It can be a never-ending series of revisions or a word count that stays stubbornly at the same number. Maybe it's a clay pot that keeps cracking in the kiln, or a pile of rejection letters that grows and grows.

However they show up, the Fives tend to give you a headache. You might respond to them with some crying time in the shower or maybe some doughnut stress-eating. Or perhaps you look around and think, "The universe is obviously trying to convey to me that I am a failure; I should give up this futile task of creative endeavor and take up plumbing or something more useful."

The secret to the Fives is that, no matter how terrible they make you feel, it just takes a bit of strategy to get past the wall. Stop using your head as a battering ram, pause for a moment, rethink what you're doing, and find a new way.

FIVE OF SWORDS

There is a situation that is hopeless, that you know is hopeless, but you've invested so much time you can't make yourself walk away. Get up, it's time to go.

FIVE OF CUPS

The disappointment of a rejection or your project's inadequacies are threatening to overwhelm you. You spend so much time focusing on what's wrong that you lose sight of the promise of everything you got right.

FIVE OF WANDS

Your article has come back covered in red ink. Or you find a moment to step back and you think, "Oh no, this is all wrong!" Scrape the canvas clean; you must start again.

FIVE OF COINS

That magazine, that clique, that artist residency doesn't want you. Instead of trying to figure out why you might be a bad fit or where you could go instead, you've chosen to lie down outside their door and wail for entry.

·•· FIVE OF SWORDS ·•·

A battlefield is shown. Swords lie strewn on the ground. One figure is collecting the swords, but the look on his face is rueful or despairing; others are walking away. Sometimes this card has a man sitting, weeping. It is unclear exactly who won this battle.

The Five of Swords is a battle with no winners. One person might gain from the experience—he is collecting the swords of his opponents. But it's not clear that he actually won, or if others simply abandoned their weapons as they were leaving the scene of battle. It is a card where one person attempts to connect with another, but instead of using their hands or their words, they use weapons. And no one wins in that scenario. Possibly a fight that must be abandoned, possibly a situation from which nothing can be gained.

In 1998 director Terry Gilliam had an idea for a film of Miguel de Cervantes's classic, *Don Quixote*. He signed up an all-star cast, led by Johnny Depp and Miranda Richardson, he had a clever twist on the story, and he was coming off of the successes of his Academy Award–nominated and financially successful films *The Fisher King* and *12 Monkeys*, and the cult-film favorite *Fear and Loathing in Las Vegas*.

But from the very beginning, the production was plagued with problems. There was a flood, and then military planes kept flying overhead, making the audio useless. The actor playing Quixote suffered an injury and had to be flown to a hospital. Then there were issues with the investors and the insurance company. The whole production had to be shut down, and the film was believed to be dead.

Gilliam would not give up. He assembled a new cast and began moving the film toward production. But again problems arose almost immediately, and actors had to quit because of scheduling conflicts. Gilliam still would not give up. He assembled a new cast and began again.

Meanwhile, he worked on other projects. His previous films, before he began working on *Don Quixote*, were all financial and artistic risks, but most paid off and became classics. *Brazil* shows up regularly on the lists of the best movies of the twentieth century, *Monty Python and the Holy Grail* is a beloved film that has been wildly influential and adapted into a successful Broadway musical, *Spamalot*. But the films that came after Gilliam refused to give up on *Don Quixote*, from *The Brothers Grimm* to *The Zero Theorem*, have been seen as self-indulgent and too cerebral with no heart. They have failed to connect with critics or audiences. It's as if his iron grip on *Don Quixote*, refusing to abandon the project, had drained the joy out of his work.

That's a Five of Swords situation. You are engaged in a fight even though you know deep down there is no way to win. But you've invested so much time, so much thought and money, that you can't give up on the dream. Your pride is such that it's not that you can't stand not winning, it's that you can't stand the idea of *losing*. It has blinded you to the reality that this is not going to work. The only thing you can do is to drop the idea wholesale and walk away. Put that energy into a new project instead of squandering it on something that isn't meant to be.

RECOMMENDED MATERIALS

Lost in La Mancha, documentary film directed by Keith Fulton and Louis Pepe

Juneteenth, book by Ralph Ellison

The War of the Roses, film directed by Danny De Vito

⋅⟶⋅ FIVE OF CUPS ⋅⟵⋅

A shrouded, mournful figure stands over two or three cups that have tipped over and are spilling their contents on the ground. He (or she— it's hard to tell) does not see two or three cups still standing behind him. (The number of spilled cups versus upright cups depends on the deck.)

The person on the Five of Cups is so busy mourning what has been lost that he cannot see what remains. There is a sense of "Don't cry over spilt milk" here, but at the same time, what is lost cannot be regained. The mourning process, however, can blind us to what is still good in our lives, and that must be considered. The Five of Cups is a warning not to get stuck and not to let disappointment ruin everything that remains.

We all, in our pursuits, will experience setbacks and disappointments. There will be rejections, people will misunderstand our work, we'll put our heart and soul into a project and watch the world respond with *meh*. The difference in how this affects us will be what we do then. Whether we get up and try again, or whether we allow our disappointment to slowly erode our ambitions and confidence.

It's easy, with this card, to get stuck in the sadness. Doubt sneaks in. We start to wonder if any of this is worth it anymore. But the card cues us: yes. There's still something left; you just need to turn around with clear eyes and see it.

The premiere of Italian composer Arrigo Boito's *Mefistofele* in 1868 was a disaster. It was his first opera, and he decided to conduct the orchestra himself, something he'd never done before. It went about as well as you can imagine. The music was chaotic, the singers missed their cues, and the audience started to riot. The reviews were vicious, and Boito was humiliated when the opera closed after only two performances. He collaborated with other composers but never finished another opera of his own.

Mefistofele was rediscovered and embraced by opera lovers. It has been sung by greats like Enrico Caruso and Luciano Pavarotti. Productions are still staged today.

It's not easy to walk away from disappointment. It is so easy to get stuck. Part of the process of the Five of Cups, however, is to mourn the loss. If we repress our feelings, just shove them down with the help of cake or booze (or cake *and* booze), or tell ourselves, "What do those jerks know, anyway?" we don't learn the lesson of why the project flopped. And if we just sink into depression, it's easy for all production to cease, as we can't regain the optimism necessary to try again. Somewhere between wallowing and repression is the way out. You cannot allow your grief to turn into depression.

The only way out is through. Feel the loss, but then eventually get over it so that you can get back to work.

RECOMMENDED MATERIALS

Mefistofele, opera by Arrigo Boito

"Daphne and Apollo," poem by Ovid

Nocturne pour violin et piano, musical composition by Lili
    Boulanger

·•· FIVE OF WANDS ·•·

Five figures stand at battle. They clash their wands together. One has dropped his wand, and he bends down to pick it up. The other fighters allow him to do this; no one attacks him in his moment of weakness.

The five fighters are in training. No one is seriously injured, no one is trying to draw blood. They are sparring in order to become better fighters. The Five of Wands represents a time of training, one that can be particularly irritating and jolting—no one becomes a great fighter without taking a few blows to the head in the process—but your life is not in danger. It is productive. You are learning from this experience.

Imagine that you're offstage in the wings. The audience is seated, the spotlight has just turned on. You are about to make your grand entrance, to step into the light and be bathed in glory, but the director pushes you back. "No, you're not ready." Again and again, you try to take the stage. Again and again, the director refuses. "You're not ready."

That is the feeling of the Five of Wands. You are ready to make your debut, you are ready for fame—or maybe you are just tired of looking at the same canvas, the same manuscript. But it keeps getting sent back for revisions. Every time you think you are finished and finally free of the project, those around you say, "Nope, try again."

It's because you haven't found excellence yet. When you're interested more in the final product than in getting everything right, a long list of things to fix might seem unfair or tedious. It is so frustrating to be told over and over that something is not right yet. But there's a reason for this. If something is going out to meet the world, you should make sure that everything is exactly the way you want it. Impatience can lead to sloppiness, and you don't want that bright spotlight to show the whole world that your shoelaces are untied and you've memorized only 75 percent of your lines.

I think of Coco Chanel, who was ruthless with her own clothing. Even as her models were about to take the stage and the clothes shown to media and buyers and clients for the first time, she was tearing out seams, restitching shoulders (she was obsessed with fitting the perfect shoulder), and sewing the models into their clothes. She would rather make the audience wait a few more moments than send out her clothes imperfect. When other people would have shrugged and said, "Good enough," she couldn't let it go.

Which is, of course, part of why she is a legend.

Creatives with this perfectionist streak—the director David Fincher, whose actors have moaned about his endless takes and retakes; the writer Henry James, whose manuscripts show obsessive rewrites and edits; the divine Coco Chanel—get reputations for being difficult or obsessed. And yet their work endures. But don't be fooled: this is a tough card to endure. So many will reach this point and then give up. Perseverance is the key, and the goal to keep shining in your mind is excellence.

RECOMMENDED MATERIALS

Zodiac, film directed by David Fincher
The Wings of the Dove, book by Henry James
Coco Avant Chanel, film directed by Anne Fontaine

·•· FIVE OF COINS ·•·

Two figures huddle in the cold outside what appears to be a church or some other form of sanctuary, but the doors are closed to them.

The Five of Coins represents alienation. Either the two figures have been forced to leave the sanctuary, or they have been denied entry. The result is the same: they are exposed to the elements, vulnerable, and will have to survive on their own. This can be due to poverty, or perhaps because of a more personal form of rejection. This card marks a time of hardship and loneliness, and a time of feeling rejected by the people who have the power to protect you.

You've been cast out. Excommunicated. That's how this card feels, like you're some kind of leper, and the people around you can't wait to stick you on an island somewhere and forget about you. You feel lost and unprotected.

161

The rejecting force can be anyone: an agent, a gallery, a collective. Your own bank account. Or maybe it's your family or your religious group. They say "You're not good enough," or "You're no longer welcome here." And there's that impulse to pound on the closed door and promise you'll do better; you'll change whatever it is that they don't like about you. Because it feels scary, this card.

When the painter Leonor Fini moved to Paris, she started hanging out with the Surrealists. Her work has a similar tone and quality: an expression of metaphor and dream logic also used by the leaders of the movement, from André Breton to Max Ernst. Their work was inspiring, and being part of the movement earned you access to gallery shows and art dealers, money and power.

But soon Fini found herself shut out of the shows and shut out of the conversation. She would meet up with the other artists and writers at the cafés, and find that no one wanted to listen to what she had to say. It was because she was a woman. Breton, the Surrealist ringleader, according to Fini, did not like women unless they were there to be pretty and nod in agreement with everything he had to say. And instead of doing just that, working quietly on her own paintings while playing along, keeping her mouth shut around Breton, Fini left the Surrealists to do her own work. Her paintings only became more complex and compelling after she left the group behind.

Collectives can be a source of inspiration. They can provide companionship and financial and emotional support. But they can also be stifling if you find yourself out of step with the rest. Life and work can be scary out in the margins, and it can be harder to find recognition, but the Five of Coins says that it's not worth trying to regain entry. The best thing is to do things your own way.

RECOMMENDED MATERIALS

The Poems of Exile, book of poetry by Ovid

Red Vision, painting by Leonor Fini

Rusalka, opera by Antonín Dvořák

THE SIXES

The Sixes are all about journeys. After the feeling of being blocked with the Fives, you have finally moved past that and are now able to make progress again.

Sometimes you'll know where you are going, and sometimes you will not. Sometimes you will be excited to be on an adventure, and other times you'll simply be plodding forward, hoping that your circumstances will change. No matter how you feel about what you're doing, however, the Sixes do imply that you are on the right track. The direction you have picked is the right one. All you have to do is keep moving forward.

To get the most out of these cards, however, you have to remember where you've been. One cannot shrug off the dark times and pretend they didn't happen. Those dark times are what led you to this point. What you learned there must be incorporated into where you are going. People say silly things when you're in pain—"It's always darkest before the dawn," et cetera, et cetera—but we are better able to appreciate the good times when we have fully accepted the dark times. It brings the creator gratitude, and it gives the creation depth.

Because of this, the Sixes are intimately tied in with the Five that preceded it, perhaps even more than the other numbered cards.

THE SIXES

SIX OF SWORDS

Maybe you're exhausted, or you might still be feeling the cruel sting of the Five of Swords, but at least you are now moving forward. Slowly but surely.

SIX OF CUPS

Following the sense of disappointment, you are able to feel joy again. Creation becomes play, and one is almost childlike.

SIX OF WANDS

Here movement feels like victory. You take what you learned and use it to overcome obstacles.

SIX OF COINS

You are able to understand now what you truly value and what you stand for. You are back in a position of strength, and you want to share what you have to give.

SIX OF SWORDS

A woman sits in a small boat. Six swords are standing upright in the boat, as if they are being used to plug holes. Her bowed head is facing the direction of where she came from, so she cannot see where they are going. The destination is either not on the card or it is not well defined.

While the card represents progress, it is not met with joy or enthusiasm. The figure has obviously been through a lot to get to this point; she seems exhausted. It is a bittersweet card. While one can be reassured that things are moving in the right direction, the pain of what came before is still fresh and might still be the primary focus.

There is some cruelty in the Five of Swords, and so often when we pull the Six, we are still feeling hurt. We might be back to work, but we can be so sad about what we just came through that we almost don't notice. Or care. "Oh, this again," we think. But when we settle in to do the work, at least we are able to do it.

It is a bit like the "Slough of Despond" in John Runyan's classic book *The Pilgrim's Progress*, first published in 1678. It is the bog, the sticky morass of feelings and fears and regrets that keeps pulling us down. Of course, in the allegory, our own sin trapped us in the muck. But there's no such thing as sin, only folly. We might have been foolish to get into the fight with ourselves or with someone else that led us into the situation of the Five. Now we're free from it, but we're still dealing with the regret.

But if you do think of it like *The Pilgrim's Progress*, the Slough of Despond is a necessary act. We're in Swords, so this is about thought and logic. The goal is to get some perspective on the feelings of regret and depression. One strives to do so only when absolutely necessary, because it can be such an unpleasant act. To really understand the source of your problems—of why you might have self-sabotaged your work in the past, of why your relationship with someone else came to blows—you have to go through some unpleasant experiences. You have to feel the consequences.

In the Christian thought that inspired Bunyan, a sinner must first understand that he has sinned in order to ask for forgiveness and be absolved. Here the only person you have to ask for forgiveness is yourself or the individual you might have hurt in the process. But the act of forgiveness and absolution is the same, and it has the same desired effect: it frees you from the Slough.

RECOMMENDED MATERIALS

The Pilgrim's Progress, book by John Bunyan

Wendy and Lucy, film directed by Kelly Reichardt

Paris, Texas, film directed by Wim Wenders

·◈· SIX OF CUPS ·◈·

Two children play near six cups full of flowers and other plant life.
The Six of Cups is a card of childhood and pleasure. In terms of
a relationship, it is often considered to be the sign of a soul mate con-
nection or perhaps a connection with someone you've known since you
were very young.

The disappointment of the Five of Cups gave a heaviness to everything for a while. One could not create because one could no longer
see the good in what he or she was doing. But with the Six, one is able
to turn around, see that not all is lost, and take joy in what remains.

It marks a moment when the act of creation becomes as exciting
as a box of crayons and a blank sheet of paper were to you when
you were a child. You could do anything you wanted. You could
make a mess, or you could try to do something more elaborate. It

almost didn't matter, because there was no such thing as failure when you were that age. You didn't mess up; you were incapable of it. At worst, it didn't quite look like you'd hoped, but now it's something even better. So your dog looks more like a dragon, who cares? Dragons can breathe fire.

A good example would be Henry Matisse's *The Cut-Outs*, those vibrantly colored, exhilarating, and liberating odes to movement and music and dance. Their boldness and their novelty are absolutely charming. They exude a sense of joy.

Matisse began working with the cut-outs near the end of his life, at a point where an artist is believed to have no innovation left. Bravery is for the young, we think too often, and one has to be brave to walk away from an acceptable way of doing something and find something new. Matisse was also blocked by a physical disability. He had become ill, and the lifelong painter was suddenly unable to work in the way he had in the past. But he could sit with a stack of paper and a pair of scissors. If you watch a video of Matisse at work with the cut-outs, he is working spontaneously, without too much control. He is having fun—you can see it on his face.

There are many times when we think we simply have nothing left. Our old ways of working no longer do the job, or we find an old source of inspiration has dried up. That's the time to consider what makes you happy and what feels like play rather than work.

RECOMMENDED MATERIALS

The Cut-Outs, series of paintings by Henri Matisse
Weetzie Bat, book by Francesca Lia Block
More Sky, book by Otto Piene
Harold and the Purple Crayon, book by Crockett Johnson

TWO OF SWORDS

TWO OF CUPS

TWO OF WANDS

TWO OF COINS

FIVE OF SWORDS

FIVE OF CUPS

FIVE OF WANDS

FIVE OF COINS

NINE OF SWORDS

NINE OF CUPS

NINE OF WANDS

NINE OF COINS

KNIGHT OF SWORDS

KNIGHT OF CUPS

KNIGHT OF WANDS

KNIGHT OF COINS

QUEEN OF SWORDS

QUEEN OF CUPS

QUEEN OF WANDS

QUEEN OF COINS

THE HIEROPHANT

TEMPERANCE

ᐧᐁᐧ SIX OF WANDS ᐧᐁᐧ

A man sits astride a horse. He is surrounded by a cheering crowd. The six wands on the card are tied up with festive wreaths and banners. He is either off on some adventure or coming back successfully.

To be literal, the man on the Six of Wands card is back on the horse again. He has overcome some sort of battle or hardship, and now he is confident and back in control. His success is celebrated by others as well. The Six of Wands can also be trying to show you that you are lording your victory or power over others. There is not a lot of humility in this card. Make sure your celebration is proportional, that you do not lose yourself in the parade.

All of that training that happened with the Five of Wands has finally paid off. You have found excellence. If you think of this in the context of a soldier, you have survived boot camp. You have been seasoned in battle. You have acquired new techniques and strategies. You are no longer just a foot soldier firing blindly and hoping for the best. You have overcome the odds and become a force to be reckoned with.

Think of someone like Alfred Hitchcock. He directed more than fifty movies in his career. He began in the 1920s, making silent and short films. He knew already what he wanted to do—his sense of atmosphere and tension were already evident—but his style was as yet unformed. In a lot of his movies in the first few decades, you can see him trying on other directors' styles, other directors' pacing, trying to find his own way.

It's not until the 1950s, thirty years after his debut, that he truly grew into his potential. Certainly he made some classics before this point, but that slick stylishness and gripping fear that we associate with Alfred Hitchcock reached their peak with a streak of classic works all within a few years of each other: *Rear Window* (1954), *Vertigo* (1958), *North by Northwest* (1959), and *Psycho* (1960).

And Hitchcock became the king of the cinematic thriller. While some of his more innovative works took awhile to be accepted, perhaps no director looms so large in our understanding of what film can do. Had he not gone through the grind of so many films, many of them mediocre or derivative in one way or another, it's doubtful he could have broken free in quite the same way.

That's the goal here: to use failures, near-misses, and lessons learned in battle, and focus on breaking through to something bigger and bolder. And then to use that success creatively, rather than immediately sitting down in your self-satisfaction, refusing to grow anymore.

RECOMMENDED MATERIALS

Vertigo, film directed by Alfred Hitchcock

The Once and Future King, book by T. H. White

·⊷· SIX OF COINS ·⊷·

A richly dressed man stands in front of two street beggars, both of whom are kneeling, with their hands outstretched. The man gives charity to one beggar but not the other. And yet his other hand holds a scale, and it is balanced perfectly.

The Six of Coins is a card about value. The man with the money is deciding what is fair, who is deserving of his assistance and his money. And he feels just—the balanced scales show that he is assessing the situation correctly. But the querent could also be the beggar, asking for help from the man who has more wealth and power than he does. This card is complicated: it asks you to question what it is you value and who you are asking for assistance. It also asks if you are sincerely in need of help, or if you are the figure who is not deserving of money. Perhaps you have more power and are less in need of charity than you'd like to admit.

You were cast out onto the margins with the Five of Coins. Maybe you couldn't get work, maybe you couldn't find acceptance. Maybe you worried you should give up entirely or that perhaps you'd starve to death before you could find your own way.

But you learn things when you have to rely solely on yourself: new ways of working, and new networks of peers and collaborators. Sometimes it takes a series of rejections for you to understand what you have to offer. And sometimes you need to learn how to value those things, so that you're not always looking for outside validation.

With the Six of Coins, you are back in contact with people in positions of power again. You have something to offer. You used your time out in the margins to hone your skills, and now you want to share what you've got. But you are not quite in a position of power yourself, so you still have to ask others for assistance and for venues to showcase your work for you. You need to make sure here that you stay true to your values.

A writer client of mine collected rejection notices from magazines for many years. He simply could not catch a break. He stopped submitting material for a while to really work on his prose style and his methods of reporting. He read works of great literature and researched the giants in his field. He understood he didn't want to take just any work available, he wanted to specialize. He wanted his work to advocate for real political change. And so his work took on a different tone, and a higher quality.

Suddenly he found himself employable again. Magazines wanted his work. But they did not always want him to write pieces that aligned with his newfound values and priorities. Because he had spent so much time out of work that he knew he could handle it, and because he had dealt with his fear of rejection, he could turn down work that didn't speak to him. He had lost his sheen of desperation. He wanted to do only work that mattered, and so he was confident in not doing work that did not.

That takes character, and grit. And that's the kind of focus that comes only when you are really clear on what you want your work to mean. The Six of Coins asks you to be true to yourself and not be swayed by offers of money or power. Your power and your strength come from within.

RECOMMENDED MATERIALS

Capital in the Twenty-First Century, book by Thomas Piketty
The Gift, book by Lewis Hyde
Untitled (Beggar in Cairo), photograph by Carlo Naya

THE SEVENS

Here, with the Sevens, we have to determine what it is we really want. This is harder than it sounds. There are the things we think that we want out of a project—fame, recognition, money—and then there are the things that will actually make us happy: satisfaction, a stray letter from a fan who really understood your intentions. These things don't always line up, and that's where conflict comes in.

Sometimes the only way to realize that the thing we've been dreaming about for so long isn't actually going to bring us joy is to get the thing and feel the disappointment. Maybe you've spent your whole life envisioning your book landing with a specific publisher. And finally: the house buys your book! Only the editor is not engaged, the cover art is terrible, and no one in publicity seems to care about you. Had you gone with a smaller publisher, with more personal attention, perhaps your book could have found a better fit, but you had fixated on a fantasy rather than looking at the reality.

Or maybe you've been writing songs and performing in very small rooms for years now, waiting impatiently for your big break. You see other people getting attention, making deals. Do you start to mold your own songs to sound more like theirs in the hopes that you too will find success?

There's also the question of what you are willing to do to get the thing that you want. Are you willing to get sneaky and take from someone else? Are you willing to stand your ground and fight hard? Or are you so uncertain about what you want that you're likely to just reach out to take anything that is offered to you?

These are the questions that the Sevens pose to us.

SEVEN OF SWORDS

If someone will not give us what we want, we might feel forced to take it.

SEVEN OF CUPS

We can suffer from delusions. What looks desirable turns out to be something of a curse, and what looks second best turns out to be the thing that makes us happy.

SEVEN OF WANDS

We have to be willing to fight for what we want.

SEVEN OF COINS

If we know what we want, then we can be patient and wait for it to come to us.

SEVEN OF SWORDS

A man is running from a town or a tent, carrying swords on his back. Some he has dropped or been forced to leave behind. The area toward which he is running is blank—an empty space.

It is unclear whether the man is carrying his own possessions or has stolen the swords from someone else. Either he is a thief trying to evade capture, or he is escaping from a terrible situation. He is leaving the safety of the city for a wild unknown. The blank space he is running toward means that he will have to construct a new world to live in, because he cannot return.

When someone doesn't give, we sometimes feel the need to take.

The creative world is full of thieves. That is not always a bad thing. Many creatives work like magpies, stealing one element from over here, matching it up with something they took from someone else over there. Some artists specialize in this, like the collage artist Hannah Hoch. Inspired by the Dada movement, she took images from magazines, advertisements, tabloids, and other noisy mass-market materials, and mixed them up to create high art. Others are not so disciplined or virtuous.

Quentin Rowan was working in a bookshop when he was offered a publishing deal for his spy thriller novels. Before his debut, *Assassin of Secrets*, was even released, he was being heralded as the next big thing. But as soon as the public got hold of his book, it became clear there was something shady going on. What first seemed like coincidental similarities between Rowan's book and books by other spy novelists were soon revealed to be outright plagiarism.

Rowan, it seemed, had stitched together his book with sentences and whole passages by other writers, such as Graham Greene and Ian Fleming, without attribution or acknowledgment. It caused a scandal, and his books were removed from shelves and destroyed.

There is emulation and then there is outright theft. There is creating something new with something old and then there is being too lazy to do the real work. Plagiarism and stealing are constant problems in the arts, from the sampling controversies in popular music to the tendency of certain journalists to become fabulists. But the impulse behind these incidents is a feeling of entitlement to something that someone else created.

Be the higher version: be Hannah Hoch, or listen to the way a musician like Beck borrows samples and stray sounds from other musicians to create something new. Stealing is the coward's way out.

RECOMMENDED MATERIALS

Cut with the Kitchen Knife Through the Beer-Belly of the Weimar Republic, photo montage by Hannah Hoch

Little Bear, etc., box construction and collage by Joseph Cornell

Untitled collages by Kara Walker

Mémoires: Structures Portantes d'Asger John, book by Guy Debord and Asger Jorn

·-◆· SEVEN OF CUPS ·◆-·

Seven cups are laid out on a bed of clouds. Each one is filled with something unique. Perhaps one holds a snake; another, jewels. One cup contains money; another, a weapon. A figure hesitates before the cups, unsure of which to take.

This is a card of many choices. And yet it is unclear if the cups contain what they seem to. Are the jewels real or fake? Is the snake poisonous or perhaps a symbol of the goddess, here to grant wisdom? The figure could be delusional, imagining things that are not really there. Or there could be so many options, but with uncertain outcomes, that he is in a state of indecision. The Seven of Cups requires a little clarity for delusion to be set aside and reason to take over.

The Seven of Cups represents the difference between fantasy and the imagination. The first is a kind of coping mechanism; a way to make yourself feel better about your circumstances. The second is a powerful tool that can lead you to great things.

With fantasy, there is no element of reality present. It's the person who dreams of becoming a rock star but never learns how to play an instrument, write songs, or join a band. He just listens to David Bowie records and imagines himself onstage in his place. This is usually born out of frustration and dissatisfaction. Perhaps he's stuck in a job he hates or feels trapped living in a small town, and so he fantasizes.

In contrast, the imagination can get you closer to actually being David Bowie. (I mean, we're all, in one way or another, trying to be David Bowie, right? We'll never make it, but it's good to have goals.) You can allow yourself to use that vision of you up on that stage to get you through the frustrating parts of developing yourself as an artist. It takes a long time to master an instrument, and there are going to be times when you think you're not making progress and you'll never get to the level of your dreams. But you can use that image—of the screaming, adoring fans; of you in control and performing your heart out—to help convince you to stick with it anyway.

If you pull the Seven of Cups, you have to ask yourself whether your idea of where you want to end up is fantasy or if it's imagination. And the only way to tell the difference is to see how much real work you're putting into your development.

RECOMMENDED MATERIALS

Brazil, film directed by Terry Gilliam
Angel, book by Elizabeth Taylor
Traumwoge, painting by Jeanne Mammen

SEVEN OF WANDS

A man fights against unknown assailants. He is using his wand as a weapon, and six other wands are lifted against him. For now, the man has the higher ground and is staying strong.

This can be a turning point in a battle, where you take the high ground and are able to fight off your opponents. The man here is in control; he is winning. But his opponents remain a mystery. It is possible, with this card, that the only person he is fighting is himself. Bad thoughts, self-defeating behavior, and so on could each be the culprit. But it can also be an outside force.

There are times when what you want is going to clash with what others want. An editor will want to take out what you feel is the heart of your novel. A mentor is going to advise you to make changes to your artwork that make you uncomfortable. Even a friend can disapprove or offer advice you find inappropriate, and you will have to defend your choices.

This takes real courage and a deep-seated belief in the work that you are doing. Be careful to note the difference, however, between arrogance and confidence. It's not going to help you to think that everything you do is perfect and that any disapproval is just people trying to cut you down. But there are moments when you'll have to face adversity, and you'll have to know, deep down, whether your work is worth defending.

When the singer-songwriter Tori Amos was recording her second album, *Under the Pink*, she clashed with her record company. Her first album had been a surprise hit, and now the label wanted her to repeat that success by making essentially the same record with a few modifications. She wanted to stretch herself, do something radical and new.

But after struggles with the company, being told that her album was no good, removing songs she believed in from the final version because someone else didn't like them, Amos found her courage. She deleted string arrangements that she thought muddled her songs and brought in her own collaborators. When the record company threatened to make more changes to the record she didn't agree with, she vowed to burn the master recordings. She believed in what she was doing, and she found the confidence to defend her choices. The album was, of course, another surprise hit.

With the Seven of Wands, those negative voices can also just be destructive thoughts. "I am not good enough." "This is not good enough." And so on. Sometimes you have to fight yourself down, too.

RECOMMENDED MATERIALS

Under the Pink, recording by Tori Amos

We Have Always Lived in the Castle, book by Shirley Jackson

⤙ SEVEN OF COINS ⤚

A man stands under a tree where coins are growing. He is not har-
vesting them, however, but waiting patiently.

The man on the Seven of Coins knows that now is not a time for
action. It would be premature. Perhaps all the specifics are not yet
known, or maybe not all of the players are in place. Either way, things
have been put into motion, and eventually they will pay off, but not
now. This card also suggests that not much work is required right now
except for patience. The work you did in the past was sufficient enough
that for now you can rest or take on new tasks.

Perhaps the best way to think about the Seven of Coins is through
the metaphor of waiting for harvest. You planted the seeds. You did
all of the maintenance, protecting the plants from bugs and bad
weather and disease. Now things are looking good and developing

in a satisfying way. The budding fruit is on the tree. And yet you know you have longer to wait. If you harvest now, you will end up with bushels of hard, sour, underripe fruit. So you remain patient. You use your extra time to do other things, think about the next season, and you wait for the ideal moment to bring in the harvest.

There are always outside forces—and internal, unhelpful thoughts as well—pressuring you to finish what you started, to publish or display the final work, to get things over and done with so that you can move on to the next thing. It can be difficult to see the virtue in sitting on something for a while, to wait for a moment you know is right. Especially now. We're in an age of instant gratification, where albums are released online the moment they are done, writing is published instantly, artwork is shared on Tumblr.

Part of that rush is the need for immediate feedback. It can be addictive to collect those Likes and Favorites, and there are so many media outlets struggling to keep up with the demand for new content that it can be easier to just slap something up there and move on to the next thing.

Pulling the Seven of Coins, though, says this is a mistake. You are not quite done; there's a refinement process that has to happen. It suggests that things are good *enough*—you could, if you really wanted to, just shrug your shoulders and say it's fine as is. But far better to wait for that moment when you know the work is its finest self and display it then.

RECOMMENDED MATERIALS

Born to Run, recording by Bruce Springsteen
Mastering the Art of French Cooking, book by Julia Child
Brooklyn Bridge, designed by John Roebling

THE EIGHTS

I always think of the Eights as being akin to the tide. Things are going out, things are coming in. The changes are subtle but real. What is important with these cards is how you respond to the changes.

In an ideal state, you don't become too attached to anything, and you allow things to come and go. When, however, are we ever really in our ideal states? We fixate, we panic, we try to control things that are beyond our control, and we get knocked down as a result. We think so much about what could be that we forget to see what *is*.

It helps to get a little perspective. Look at the situation in the long term. Are you completely satisfied with where you are now? If not, then things will have to change somehow. So best to think about it in the sense of how you'll feel six months or a year from now rather than how you feel about it right now.

The Eights can be very emotional cards. Think of Strength for the ideal response, a kind of quiet managing rather than a wrestling match. Be sure to take good care of yourself: get enough sleep, don't overindulge, stay hydrated. It's easier to deal with strong emotions when you are strong physically.

EIGHT OF SWORDS

All of the uncertainty has led to a state of fear. You respond by feeling helpless and waiting for someone else to tell you what to do.

EIGHT OF CUPS

A realization sets in that what you have is not enough. You have to go out and look for what it is you want.

EIGHT OF WANDS

Something is coming in, fast. Your job is simply to try to respond to this new information or new offer or new ideas.

EIGHT OF COINS

Instead of thinking about what is to come, you focus on what is directly in front of you.

EIGHT OF SWORDS

A woman stands encircled by swords. She is bound and blind-folded. Her blindfold, however, is loose, as is the rope around her. But the woman makes no move to free herself.

The woman on the Eight of Swords card is awaiting rescue from an outside force. Rather than removing her own blindfold and untying herself, she is waiting for someone to come by and do this for her. Whether because of past trauma or simply a white-knight fantasy, the result is the same: she is going to wait for a very long time.

The problem with experiencing a series of setbacks is that we can spend all of our time expecting the next one. After a series of rejections or maybe a series of failed experiments, after failing time and time again to get it right, we lose all confidence. Doubt sets in.

And so begins a time when we are certain that we can't do anything right. We don't trust our own judgment, and we certainly don't feel up to starting all over again. We pretend like we can't, both to ourselves and to other people. "Nope," we say to our friends and colleagues, "I can't possibly make it up that hill one more time. You go on without me. I'll just lie down here; it'll be fine."

Of course, half the reason we think or say things like that is because we want someone to rescue us. To dust us off, and tell us how smart and important and talented we are. Or we want someone to tell us what to do, so that we don't have to take responsibility for our own decisions. It's an understandable response to failure, but that doesn't mean it's a good place to stay stuck. The only thing to do when you have the Eight of Swords is to save yourself. No one else is coming for you. You have only yourself to rely on. So it's either save yourself or quit entirely. Which is it going to be?

The painter Lee Krasner was told over and over again that her work wasn't worth much. Part of that was from being a woman at an art school run by men. But it repeated after that when she married the much more successful painter Jackson Pollock. Her work lived in his shadow. She began obsessively destroying her own artwork when she did not feel it was good enough. For a while, so much of what she created instantly ended up in shreds on the floor, any progress she made was instantly erased, until it was like she wasn't moving at all.

But Krasner pulled herself out of the destructive habit, almost by accident. As she looked down at her destroyed canvases, she saw how well the smaller pieces of the different paintings worked together. She began to collage the pieces into wholly new works. The destruction became an act of creation.

You must do the same when you pull the Eight of Swords. You have to find a way to create again.

RECOMMENDED MATERIALS

Andromeda, painting by Gustave Moreau

Voyage in the Dark, book by Jean Rhys

Saint George Killing the Dragon, painting by Bernat Martorell

Bird Talk, painting by Lee Krasner

·•· EIGHT OF CUPS ·•·

Eight cups are arranged along the ground, but there is a gap in the line of cups. One cup is obviously missing. A figure has wandered off into the distance, obviously looking for the lost cup. It is night, the moon is out, but it is not giving off a lot of light.

The missing cup represents our dissatisfaction. There is something missing for us in this situation, some emotional connection, and so we have to leave what we have and go searching for what we lack. There is nothing wrong with the eight cups on the card—they are all intact, they are all upright. But the gap is still noticeable. The figure has wandered off at night, indicating that not even he knows exactly what he is looking for. It might be an arduous journey, but he is committed.

Sometimes we have to abandon work when it is no longer satisfying to us. This is not easy, as we invest so much into what we do: time, energy, emotional attachment, hopes. To admit then that something is not working and to walk away from it, that requires great strength.

It can almost be like leaving a relationship. It's not simply the memories of the good of what you were doing, it's the imagined future that you also have to separate from. We take on work because of the glittering horizon: our ideas of how it'll be when it is finished. And it's not just our work but our actual selves that we pour into what we do. Leaving it, admitting that the end result is no longer worth it, is very difficult.

The thing that cues us that this is what has to happen is a sense of dissatisfaction. Often we have to feel dissatisfied and anxious and terrible for a long time before we'll admit to the truth that we should be doing something else. Søren Aabye Kierkegaard, the nineteenth-century Danish philosopher, wrote about how anxiety is a necessary emotion that should be listened to—it is cuing you that change is needed. It is a feeling of uprooting, which is unsettling, but it prepares you for action. Often one must feel the anxiety and the instability in order to make great changes.

So it's time to leave what you've been doing and wander around in the dark for a while. You have to go find what does actually satisfy you. It is the start of a journey, and the thing you are searching for won't be obvious immediately. That's the upside to this card: the potential for something new that you will connect with and feel good about. But first comes the sadness of walking away.

RECOMMENDED MATERIALS

Winterreise, song cycle by Franz Schubert
The Meaning of Anxiety, book by Rollo May
Home for the Holidays, film directed by Jodie Foster

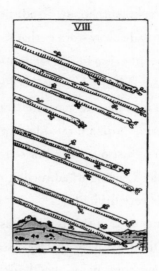

EIGHT OF WANDS

Eight wands fall from the sky. They appear to have been thrown with great force and are now coming in for a landing.

Both the figure who threw the wands and the figure who will ostensibly catch the wands are unknown to us, meaning this is almost an impersonal card. The wands—inspiration, passion, religious feeling— come entirely from the outside; they did not come from us. These are ideas or messages of some sort that are dropping in on us from we know not where. It will be our job to incorporate these ideas.

We need input. Not all of the best ideas originate in us. We occasionally need an outside source to tell us what it is we should be doing.

The energy of the Eight of Wands has almost nothing to do with us. It is something descending upon us from above. This is not always easy for us to take. We like to think of ourselves as autonomous creative geniuses; that our ideas will obviously be the best. After all, who knows us better than us? Who knows what we're good at, what we're capable of, what will make us happy better than the person actually inhabiting our bodies? No one! So we know what is best for us.

Not necessarily. We all need money. And so when we take on an assignment for the cash, we can feel a bit like sell-outs. We can feel like we are debasing ourselves for the sake of survival. We think of it as our lesser work.

But consider someone like the American painter John Singer Sargent. He subsidized his original work by painting portraits for money. A man would hire him to paint his wife or his daughter, or a socialite who wanted to be immortalized would pay him to do the honors. Certainly, some of those paintings are clearly mediocre. You can tell his heart was not in some of them. But many of Sargent's finest and best-known works today are his portraits. These were works that were not his idea, but he created great art out of what might otherwise have been simply a financial transaction.

So don't resist other people's ideas. Don't snobbishly turn something away simply because it did not originate with you. Don't think you're better than your assignment. Listen to what is being said and see it for what it is: a great opportunity.

RECOMMENDED MATERIALS

Lady Agnew of Lochnaw, painting by John Singer Sargent

Sistine Chapel ceiling, fresco painting by Michelangelo

Review of A. A. Milne's *The House at Pooh Corner*, *The New Yorker*, by Dorothy Parker

⊷ EIGHT OF COINS ⊷

A man is seated in a small studio. On his table are eight identical coins. It is clear that he has crafted these coins. He is still at work on one of them. Outside his window in many versions of this card, you can see the castle of a walled city.

The man in the Eight of Coins is entirely absorbed in his work. The job here is to create excellence and consistency. His thoughts are not on the fame or money that will come; they are only on doing a very good job. The castle outside his window means he is isolated in his work; it is not the time to take the work to the market. This is a card of diligence and craft.

In the medieval era, artists were expected to reproduce work, not create new work. The important thing was consistency, not individuality. The Catholic Church needed icons of religious figures, and they had to be instantly recognizable to the congregation. Each figure looked consistent: Saint Lucia would be carrying her own eyes; Saint Catherine, a wheel; the Virgin Mary would be in the same pose in almost every image. Artists, then, worked within these constraints, creating the same figure again and again throughout their careers.

That is how the Eight of Coins feels. It's not about individual glory—at least, not yet. You are repeating the same task until you get really good at it. Until you are able to perform consistently. This is a card of craft, not of art.

Even Pablo Picasso, before he became *Picasso*, had to draw life studies and understand the anatomy of the human body as he was learning. You have to have the basics down before you can innovate. And here there's a focus on the task at hand, not on where this is all going to lead. You're doing this to hone your skills, not because it's going to make you rich or famous.

If you're impatient, the Eight of Coins can feel like boot camp. You're not using live rounds, you're just running drills—there's no real action. There's no glory in the Eight of Coins. But you're not doing it for the glory, you are doing it to learn. In that way, it's similar to the Five of Wands, except here it's a solitary process; there's no outside figure telling you what you're doing wrong or to start over.

The medieval painter Simone Martini painted icons endlessly, just like everyone else. When a church's painting had rubbed away or started to flake, he would just create another one exactly like the painting being replaced. But then he started to get really good.

His work took on new flourishes, and he became quite innovative for the era. Even the small variations he added gave the work great depth. Martini is now considered one of the masters of the era.

You have to be willing to put aside your ego and just learn for a while. The payoff is worth it.

RECOMMENDED MATERIALS

Andrei Rublev, film directed by Andrei Tarkovsky
The Annunciation, painting by Simone Martini
Self-Portrait, painting by Chuck Close

THE NINES

The Nines appear when we have to face a situation on our own. No teachers, no mentors, no editors or friends or lovers can help us now. Depending on the suit, that can either be a cause for celebration (the Nine of Cups is often referred to as the big "yes" card), or it can be awful (the Nine of Swords usually appears only after a panic attack and a sleepless night or two). Either way, these are decisions we must make for ourselves.

There are times when we need outside input in order to gain perspective on what's going on. A person who is detached and not emotionally invested in our process can often see things we can't see, both weaknesses and strengths. But the Nines say that either the outside voice isn't there for us or we don't need it.

An artist must find a balance between self-reliance and looking for approval from others. If you are too insular, your work can become self-indulgent, airless. However, if you are always looking for other people to tell you when you are doing good work, your work can become bland from trying to appeal to the widest possible audience.

The Nines direct you to any potential imbalances between these two poles and help you figure out how to correct them. Are you closing yourself off from valuable criticism? Do you need to find pride in your own work? These are the cards to help you figure that out.

NINE OF SWORDS

Giving our fears enough time and space can turn thoughts into monsters.

NINE OF CUPS

Alone in our splendor.

NINE OF WANDS

You're not only standing alone but also barring entry to anyone else. Are you putting on a good defense, or are you being overly defensive?

NINE OF COINS

This is the moment when all of the training finally pays off, and you're allowed onto the stage to show the world what you've got.

◆— NINE OF SWORDS —◆

*A man sits up in bed at night, clutching his head in pain or despair.
Nine swords line the adjacent wall.*

*The Nine of Swords can be the insomnia card, or the anxiety card.
The man's thoughts are keeping him awake. He is totally alone. Even
if there were someone sleeping next to him, when fear overwhelms us,
we are alone.*

This is the awake-again-at-four-in-the-morning-replaying-all-the-ways-you-are-a-failure-and-will-always-be-a-failure card.

Anxiety and self-doubt have scuttled many promising projects.
They've led to manuscripts being tossed in the fire, canvases slashed,
tapes erased. The nineteenth-century Russian writer Nikolay Vasil-yevich Gogol claimed the devil made him burn the second part
of his masterpiece *Dead Souls*, and it's not for nothing that artists

have portrayed self-destructive thoughts and impulses as demons and devils for centuries. Who knows how many more great books there would be in the world had writers not given up even before putting pen to paper?

Search Google Images for Martin Schongauer's engraving *The Temptation of St. Anthony*. That is how that card feels: like you're being battered and pulled apart by demons, except those demons are your negative thoughts. They're coming from you, not from any outside force. If we talked to other people the way we talk to ourselves—"You're not good enough, nothing you do matters," and so forth—we'd be deeply ashamed.

It is helpful to remember that these anxious thoughts are not supported by reality. If we were able to get a little perspective, a little emotional distance, we could see the potential in what we are doing rather than just the deficiencies. We also let outside concerns, like our desire for fame or our need for money, drive us when we're working.

The best thing you can do with the Nine of Swords is to try to turn off your brain as much as possible. Find a way to stop interfering with your work and get back to a place of flow. Allow yourself to mess up, and quiet the concerns of ego and money that are simply adding to the pressure. Easier said than done, I know!

At the very least, try to introduce some reality to your fears. You are not doomed forever because you are a week past deadline, nor will you starve to death just because you messed up something and have to start over. Ask someone for an outside opinion, talk to someone about your difficulties. The Nine of Swords is a dark card, so switch on the light and see that those monsters you created in your mind are really just tree branches scratching against the window.

RECOMMENDED MATERIALS

The Temptation of St. Anthony, engraving by Martin Schongauer
Insomnia, film directed by Erik Skjoldbjærg
The Nightmare, painting by Henri Fuseli

·•· NINE OF CUPS ·•·

A content, satisfied-looking man or woman sits alone in a room, surrounded by nine cups.

The cups represent a kind of bounty. Although this person is not sharing, he or she does not appear to be stingy, simply happy. It is a card the represents self-sufficiency. The figure obviously earned these nine cups and is now going to enjoy the fruits of his or her labor.

Think of the Nine of Cups as the card of the spinster. Not the sad, eternally tormented Miss Havisham kind of spinster, but rather the bombshell spinsters in old movies and the spinsters in Henry James novels. The spinster who has her own bank account and travels the world unencumbered by a husband or someone else's desires.

Because the Nine of Cups is about finding satisfaction all on your own. As an artist, that means you don't need to look to an outside source to tell you your work is good. This is harder than it sounds. So often we need someone else to grant us permission to feel good about ourselves. We look for outside validation from friends, peers, lovers, mentors. "Tell me this is good," we say, handing over our most precious work. "Validate me. Tell me I'm worthy." And because we have a bad habit of mixing up our selves and our work, that rejection or that acceptance can feel like it's about *us* rather than something we created. A good word and we feel invincible. A bad one can send us into a tailspin of depression.

One has to be careful, though, not to let this devolve into puffed-up arrogance and become an "Everything I do is brilliant and must be seen by the whole world!" kind of jerk. There are writers who refuse to be edited because they think every word they write is as precious as a diamond. (They're almost always wrong.) There are artists who respond to constructive criticism by spitting fire. This is just as obnoxious as the person who needs constant positive feedback to keep going.

When this card shows up, it's a sign that one has to achieve a kind of critical eye, to be able to scan one's own work and see not only any weaknesses but also its good points. Being satisfied with your own work means that you know how to listen to outside opinions but also know when they should be disregarded. It makes you steadier in your aim and truer to your own self.

RECOMMENDED MATERIALS

Auntie Mame, film directed by Morton DaCosta
Mrs. Craddock, book by W. Somerset Maugham
Washington Square, book by Henry James

·--◆ NINE OF WANDS ◆--·

Eight wands are planted in a line, like a wall or a fence. A man, badly injured, stands in front of them, clutching a wand of his own. He is guarding them. He has no compatriots, and it is unclear if the enemy is close or even coming at all.

The injured man has recently been in battle. That battle is either over or has paused. The man has decided to arrange the wands as a kind of boundary to the territory he either won or is defending. Because the enemy is unseen, though, it is possible that this man is not under attack. Perhaps he could leave his post, see to his wounds, get some rest. But instead, he is anticipating the next siege. He is defensive, but it's unclear whether that is necessary.

Most of us resist change. It's scary, it's uncertain, it tends to be painful. And yet without it, we risk becoming stubborn and stale. Old-fashioned, even.

Composer Igor Stravinsky lived during an interesting time for classical music. The early twentieth century saw a powerful shift happening, from orchestral music to jazz. While all of the elites, the critics and the tastemakers, were still devoted to what was happening in symphony halls and opera houses, growing numbers of people were embracing the more free-form and less stodgy jazz music.

Many of Stravinsky's peers became snobs. Jazz music was trash, noise, they huffed. But real geniuses, like Duke Ellington and Glenn Miller, were innovating and producing great work, and the audiences were responding to it in droves. So that snobbery was not based on an accurate understanding of what the music was. It was born from defensiveness.

We get defensive when we fear we are about to lose our power or when we begin to fear that maybe we made some wrong decisions. We use that defensiveness to protect ourselves from doubt, from the creeping fear that we are about to become obsolete. You see it in writers who are afraid of the internet, and so make grand proclamations about how it's all a waste of time, that great work can't come from someone who writes online. You see it in the painfully small audiences at contemporary classical music performances, most of which is so obscure and abstract as to be unlistenable.

Stravinsky did not fear jazz music. He absorbed it. He learned from it, and he changed his own music as a result. Which is why he was loved by jazz musicians such as saxophone virtuoso Charlie Parker, and also why he stayed relevant and productive until his death in 1971. And his peers who scoffed that jazz music was just a fad and unworthy of public attention? No one remembers them anymore.

RECOMMENDED MATERIALS

"Preludium for Jazz Band," composed by Igor Stravinsky

La Place de la Concorde Suisse, book by John McPhee

The Phaedrus, book by Plato

·•· NINE OF COINS ·•·

A woman, standing in a garden, surrounded by nine coins. A falcon, like the type royalty once used for hunting, perches on her shoulder or hand.

The falcon, now tamed, is the unconscious side of yourself—the darker side—which is now under the woman's control. The dark side has become useful; it can be sent off to hunt. Thus, the woman can retain her dignity. Her hands remain clean; the falcon does the dirty work for her. She is poised, decorated with the Coins she earned with her labor, and all of her feral parts have been domesticated. It is a card of excellence, of focus, and of self-control.

The little girl falls in love with the ballerina on the stage. She is so ethereal, her movements are so effortless. "That is who I want to be," says the little girl.

Then she's introduced to ballet class. Rather than floating around on a cloud, she must practice the smallest of movements again and again and again. She must strengthen her body, she must do the same spin until she feels like her head is going to fall off. "But this isn't *dancing*," she thinks. A lot of children quit dance, or music, or anything else at this moment, when they realize that it is going to take a lot of hard work.

The Nine of Coins is the payoff for a lot of hard work. It indicates the moment when you go from practicing and learning to actually *dancing*. It shows you the freedom that comes once you have attained excellence or completeness.

What it takes to get there is, of course, all of that rote, boring, repetitive work. The Russian prima ballerina Anna Pavlova, one of the greatest dancers who ever lived, was not satisfied with simply going to dance class. She sought out Russia's most renowned teachers and took extra classes with them. She developed a new kind of pointe shoe because the old one didn't suit her weird arches. And despite being teased for her long limbs and her unusual technique, she practiced obsessively until she had every movement down.

And once she got onstage, all of that painful training paid off. Her movements were effortless. She reached the Nine of Coins stage where a person gets so good at the basics that she transcends them. It is excellence through enduring all of the boring, tedious stuff. It requires patience and hard work, but the payoff is worth it.

RECOMMENDED MATERIALS

Baryshnikov Live at Wolf Trap, DVD by Mikhail Baryshnikov
Judy at Carnegie Hall, DVD by Judy Garland
I Dreamed I Was a Ballerina, book by Anna Pavlova

THE TENS

We've reached the end. All of the Tens represent a conclusion of some kind. And as any good reader knows, there are a lot of ways to end a play. Bloody death with bodies strewn everywhere? A happily-ever-after wedding? Not all of the endings will be what you wish for, but at least it's over, and one can begin again.

With the Tens, it's important to accept the end. You can fight against the circumstances and the way things are ending, but you can't keep looking for something that is no longer there. Stop going to a well that is dry. Start again, build a new well.

Endings are naturally bittersweet, even when they're happy. It can be sad to put something on the shelf and walk away. And they can make you feel a little lost. "Now what? I spent the last five years of my life on this one thing, and now what do I do?"

Anything you want.

So take the Tens with grace, and deal with the ending any way you wish. Mourn if it's sad, celebrate if it's happy. And then rest up, because it's all just going to start up again soon.

TEN OF SWORDS

A nasty end, bloody and violent. You fought for something, and you lost. This is the darkest of the Tens.

TEN OF CUPS

Satisfaction and celebration. The whole community comes out to celebrate your good deeds.

TEN OF WANDS

Burnout and exhaustion. You have to put an end to something because it's just become too difficult and overwhelming.

TEN OF COINS

You've achieved a happy, comfortable stability.

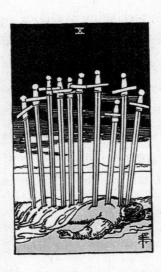

TEN OF SWORDS

A man lies on the ground. Ten swords are stuck in his back, and there is blood on the ground. The man's face is turned toward the horizon. He is either already dead or quickly becoming so.

With ten swords, the man is destroyed under their weight. The swords represent thoughts, ideas, fears. They are not useful because there are too many of them. The Ten of Swords is a card of defeat. There is nowhere else for his thoughts to go; they have destroyed him and his potential. The hope of the card is the gaze toward the horizon. His act of surrender can lead to a new beginning, but first the defeat must be felt.

Okay, let's not pussyfoot around here. The Ten of Swords is the card of failure.

And you can use any New Agey mumbo jumbo to try to soften

the blow: "There's no such thing as failure" or whatever. Tell that to the devastating depression that can descend with this card. Tell those feelings there's no such thing as failure.

It *is*, of course, true—in the grand scheme of things. Unless you actually die in the attempt, like a sad Ernest Shackleton, the British polar explorer, there's always the ability to take what you learned and try again. Wiping out, falling flat on your face, can be a good motivating force. You take that humiliation and you think, "I will prove you all wrong."

Even Shackleton, who died of a heart attack, heavily in debt, on his last Antarctic voyage in 1922, was vindicated by history. On a previous expedition in 1915, his ship, the *Endurance*, became trapped in the ice, forcing him and his men to survive the harsh Arctic weather for more than a year. They had to eat their dogs to keep from starving. But now he's heralded as a genius; a man who persevered despite desperate odds.

Which does not necessarily make this card any easier to take, I know. "Oh, look! You're dead, and you left your wife in financial ruin, but in a hundred years they'll make a documentary about you!" That's the hard part of this card. Even if you know that the failure will be redeemed in the end, even if you know that ultimately it is an important part of your process, it feels like absolute hell.

Surrender to the failure. Allow it to be. Do whatever difficult emotional work you have to do to come to terms with the failure and then get ready to try again.

RECOMMENDED MATERIALS

"Rock 'n' Roll Suicide," recording by David Bowie

Child with Toy Hand Grenade in Central Park, photograph by
    Diane Arbus

The Liver Is the Cock's Comb, painting by Arshile Gorky

Ariel, book of poetry by Sylvia Plath

·-◆ TEN OF CUPS ◆-·

A family stands together, holding hands and dancing. Above them is a rainbow, with ten cups arrayed within the arc.

The family is connected and loves one another. The rainbow indicates a happy ending: a promise of prosperity to come. It is an emotion shared among the closest of allies: either a supportive community or a family or a group of friends.

This is the traditional happily-ever-after card. It can be an end to a project that deserves celebration. Invite the family over, open the champagne, and raise a glass to your great success.

Thematically, though, this is the fairy-tale card. It's the ending that ties up everything neatly, that solves everyone's problems. Evils are vanquished, peace reigns, and love is treasured. These endings can feel a little sarcastic, right? Great art works in dark tones. Happiness is too boring and too unbelievable to inspire geniuses.

And yet that is not to say there is no darkness in the fairy tale. Of course there is. Children are eaten by wolves and witches, mothers turn out to be enemies instead of protectors, a curse casts a dark pall over the entire kingdom. But it ends on an uplifting note, when everything difficult and evil has been overcome.

The English novelist Jane Austen ended many of her books neatly, with a wedding. It is the fairy-tale ending. But because it is hard-won, the reader doesn't have to roll her eyes. It's never the couple who falls in love easily and for whom everything goes swimmingly. That would be boring. It's the couple for whom nothing works, who must face down adversity, who must be brave and forthright in order to win the love they deserve. That's an ending worth cheering.

When you pull the Ten of Cups about your project, you might want to look at it through this lens. Is it too sickly sweet—almost sarcastic in its cheeriness? Or are you trying to make it dark simply because you think that's more important, and does it deserve a little lightening up?

Let your happiness be your muse for a while, rather than your pain.

RECOMMENDED MATERIALS

Sense and Sensibility, film directed by Ang Lee

From the Beast to the Blonde: On Fairy Tales and Their Tellers, book by Marina Warner

As You Like It, play by William Shakespeare

·-· TEN OF WANDS ·-·

A hunched-over figure is carrying ten wands. They are so heavy and unwieldy that they block his view of where he's going.

The man in the Ten of Wands is carrying more than he should. By burdening himself with all of the wands at once, he is hindering his own progress. You get the sense that if he put down some of the wands and took multiple trips, it might take longer, but he would be more successful. Or if he carried the wands in a different arrangement, he could see where he was going. As it is, though, the burden has become overwhelming. If one is going to carry on, adjustments will have to be made.

Burnout is an interesting word, and it is very fitting for the Ten of Wands. The Wands represent fire, everything that excites us and gives us pleasure. But too much excitement can lead to exhaustion, and too much fire can lead to burnout.

If we do not figure out how to ground ourselves, how to be practical rather than only passionate, we can sometimes run into trouble. Our health fails, we lose our way. What was once vitally important to us becomes only a source of misery. Where we once dedicated ourselves wholeheartedly, we now turn away. You see it all of the time with people who run on passion as if it were a fuel: emergency room doctors who work eighteen-hour days only to have to retire to a quiet private practice; aid workers who are used to working in war zones until one day they simply can't anymore. If our passions are not made manageable, we can't sustain our energy over a long span of time. We're forced to quit.

Many creative spirits have suffered from this: from Arthur Rimbaud, who gave up poetry to become a merchant; to composer Franz Schubert, whose passionate love life killed him off from syphilis at a young age. A slew of rock stars have burned out young, dying from suicide, drugs, and alcohol. Or they simply couldn't sustain their creativity over a long career, and after one or two brilliant albums were never really heard from again.

The Ten of Wands, then, can show up as a warning. It also asks you to interrogate the dark side of passion. How the trajectory of the Wands, which starts off so promising, so exciting, ends up in such a disappointing state.

RECOMMENDED MATERIALS

A Season in Hell, prose poem by Arthur Rimbaud
Horses, recording by Patti Smith
A Passage to India, book by E. M. Forster

· TEN OF COINS ·

A group of people enter a walled garden or city. The Coins are arranged so that they are available to anyone. There is a quiet contentment to this card.

The men and women on this card are sharing their bounty. This is a card of community and of generosity. But note that there is a wall, so there is a strict boundary. Only certain people can gain admittance and take part in the wealth.

The Ten of Coins is a community. It's wealth that can be spread around. By wealth, I don't mean money, although it can mean that. It's generosity of spirit, of attention, of assistance. It's a group of people who can come to one another's aid, and offer support and fraternity. They bring one another stability.

There have been many great communities in the art world, from the Paris scene during the rise of the Impressionists, to the New York intellectual circles after World War II. People inspired one another, they published one another, they formed movements and opened galleries and ate and drank together. They kept one another company.

In our age of online communities, these circles no longer have to be centered on a physical location. You can form writing groups with people all over the world. Twitter and Facebook have become the new parlors and cafés.

But even in the early twentieth century, international communities were forming, thanks to the little magazines. During the modernist era, dozens of these little arts and literature journals sprang up, run by dedicated editors in it for the love of the work. Margaret Anderson formed *Little Review* in the United States, but her poetry editor, Ezra Pound, lived in Italy; her regular contributor James Joyce lived in Paris; and other helpers were in London.

That collection of writers, editors, and artists helped shape modernism, a revolution in art. They worked together and supported one another, and the magazine helped spread the word. They were able to gain a larger audience together than they ever would have been able to separately, as their work was so eccentric and different from everything that had come before. They inspired one another.

This card asks you to find your community. Not only to help you in your work but also to help others in theirs. It makes the process of creative work, often carried out alone in rooms with shut doors, much less lonely.

RECOMMENDED MATERIALS

The Strange Necessity, book by Margaret Anderson

L'Album des Six, suite of six piano pieces by Georges Auric, Louis Durey, Arthur Honegger, Darius Milhaud, Francis Poulenc, and Germaine Tailleferre

Zero: Countdown to Tomorrow, 1950s–60s, book by Valerie Hillings and Daniel Birnbaum

THE PAGES

The Pages are the youngest of the court cards. Their youth does not necessarily have anything to do with their physical age. It's more about behavior and outlook. There's a kind of excitement and boundless energy about the Pages. They are the most immature, and so occasionally they can be more chaotic than helpful.

But they are the start of something new. You need the spring of optimism at the beginning of a new adventure—otherwise you'll never pack your bag and be on your way. The Page provides that optimism, but he's going to have to mature a bit to commit to seeing the project all the way through.

Pages are also messengers, and so he can show up with opportunities and ideas that have to be worked through. They are more inspiring than dedicated to work: they can be someone who says something amazing that sparks an idea in your head, and then he disappears while you go to work.

The Pages will start more projects than they finish, and they're always coming up with new ideas that don't necessarily go anywhere. If you're the Page in a tarot reading, it might be a cue that it's time for you to grow up a little and see a project to completion for a change. But if someone else is the Page, you had better listen to what he is saying, because he is here to bring you some kind of message.

PAGE OF SWORDS

This Page can show up like a fly buzzing in your ear. The annoyance of it wakes you up and moves you to action. It might be an argument or a puzzle that draws an idea out of you.

PAGE OF CUPS

This is a message about love or about a deep emotional connection. The Page of Cups is most likely to be a muse, someone who inspires a work but never actually becomes your partner.

PAGE OF WANDS

This is the start of a great adventure. It might be an opportunity to travel, the beginning of an affair, or a religious conversion. Something that puts you on the path toward something very exciting; something that lights you up.

PAGE OF COINS

The Page of Coins will provide you with some sort of hint for how to turn your idea into reality; how to invest your resources for the biggest payoff later.

PAGE of SWORDS.

⸺•·⸺ PAGE OF SWORDS ⸺·•⸺

A young man holds aloft a sword almost as large as he is.

The Page of Swords is a student, either in reality or in metaphor. He or she works with words, thoughts, ideas, communication, but has yet to develop any real command over these air qualities. This card represents honesty and clarity but also, on occasion, trouble. It could represent someone who spurs you on with discomfort and irritation rather than with command.

Not everyone has it in them to write a book. That's what the Page of Swords can represent: a great idea with no outlet. Maybe it's lack of discipline, maybe it's lack of free time, but the idea stays only an idea, unless it meets up with the type of person who does have the necessary attributes to write a book.

So we have someone like Esther Murphy, a brilliant woman

who was always talking about the books she was going to write but never actually wrote a single one in all of her life. She was always surrounded by writers, but she never seemed to figure out how to do it herself. Maybe she was too social and didn't know what to do with herself when alone. Perhaps she was too much of a perfectionist and tore up every false start. She had great ideas, but they never found form.

We should, then, ask what are the ethics of taking an idea from someone else—someone who is not likely to use it? We take our ideas from people all the time. Pages of Swords show up everywhere. Someone will say something in line at the grocery store, and it sticks in your brain. Or you decide to modernize a storyline from a myth or a fairy tale. Or you hear distorted music from a passing car, and it shifts itself into a new line of melody. We're always grabbing things from our environment and then using them to create.

That's different, though, than taking an *idea*, and the ethics there are shaky. Certainly Zelda Fitzgerald acted as muse to her husband F. Scott, but she was trying to be a writer herself. Many of his most memorable lines were actually things that Zelda had originally said or written. F. Scott felt entitled to take her writings to use in his own writings. Most of the time, this happened without her permission. That's a morally dubious arrangement.

At the same time, Zelda did not have her husband's discipline. She had great ideas, a few great lines, but she was unable to form them into a cohesive work. She had one novel, *Save Me the Waltz*, which was heavily edited by F. Scott because he was furious that she would try to write something about their marriage on her own. Nonetheless, even if we factor in the controlling husband, Zelda was not much of a writer. And without her husband, many of her thoughts, ideas, and witty lines would have been lost to us.

The Page of Swords might present you with an idea, but it's up to your own moral center to determine whether you can take it. And if you yourself are the Page, then it is time for you to take the great idea you are bursting with and figure out a way to turn it into a real thing. It might be time for you to mature into one of the higher court cards.

RECOMMENDED MATERIALS

Tender Is the Night, book by F. Scott Fitzgerald
All We Know: Three Lives, book by Lisa Cohen
Save Me the Waltz, book by Zelda Fitzgerald

PAGE of CUPS.

⟶ PAGE OF CUPS ⟵

A young man or woman stands holding a cup. A small fish leans out of the cup. The two appear to be in conversation.

The fish on the Page of Cups card represents our intuitive self. The parts of us that came from the sea; the very old, pre-language part of ourselves that developed before we crawled out of the water and onto land, before we developed our marvelous brains. The Page of Cups is in conversation with that part of herself. She is connected with her intuition and in touch with her feelings. Often this card represents a new love interest. But it mostly suggests that deep down, you already know the answer to the question you are asking. You merely have to uncover it.

Not everyone we fall in love with is good for us. That should be clear by the time a person reaches adulthood. But not every failed love affair is a waste of time, either. Maybe the beloved left you in torment, led you to financial or emotional ruin, maybe he drove you to drink. But I bet you got a bunch of good stories out of it.

The Page of Cups can therefore be the muse. It's more about a message of love than love itself, more of a quaking vulnerability than a solid and stable relationship. The Page of Cups gets us at our core. We know this person is *ours* in some way. It's why people make up stories about having known a person in a past life. Somehow we know a person before we've met them. Then they show up, and we wonder how we ever did without them. Even if those feelings are not returned.

William Butler Yeats remembered the exact moment he met his muse, the Irish revolutionary Maud Gonne. She was like a shining vision from another dimension. She didn't really remember meeting him; she thought it was at one party or another. The pain of the unrequited love is surprisingly inspirational. Gonne never returned his feelings, and she turned down his many offers of marriage, but some of the greatest poetry of the twentieth century came out of that arrangement.

There's also Jeanne Duval, who inspired not only the nineteenth-century French poet Charles-Pierre Baudelaire but also the painter Édouard Manet. Duval was Haitian, and so not an acceptable candidate for marriage in polite French society. She was also an actress and a singer, not respectable vocations for the time. But wives do not make good muses. They are around too much; there is not enough mystery about them. Mistresses, on the other hand, who torture you with their independence, who are elusive and strange, who taunt you with the knowledge that you do not know where they go when they are not with you, nor with whom. That kind of stuff drags great poetry out of a person.

Of course, muses have lives of their own. The great muse to many of the photographers of the early twentieth century, Lee Miller, decided to pick up a camera of her own. She became a great war photographer, no longer just posing for others. But for your purposes, the Page is here to deliver the inspiration. It's up to you what you do with it.

RECOMMENDED MATERIALS

Lee Miller, photograph by Man Ray

Flowers of Evil, book of poetry by Charles-Pierre Baudelaire

The Gonne-Yeats Letters, 1893–1938, book edited by
Anna MacBride White and A. Norman Jeffares

·- PAGE OF WANDS -·

A young man or woman stands in a wild landscape, holding a wand as if it were a walking stick. No supplies are carried, and yet no civilization is in sight.

The Page of Wands marks the beginning of a new adventure. It's unclear, so far, where one is going, and that makes it difficult to prepare. The Page of Wands is optimistic and enthusiastic, almost to the point of being foolhardy. The enthusiasm outweighs, by far, the Page's ability to complete the task successfully. He or she will have the opportunity to learn along the way, however.

The Page of Wands wants a big adventure, and he runs off to have it without thinking much about preparation, destination, or what he'll need along the way. Unfortunately for the Page, that's how

233

you get killed on adventures, forgetting to bring essentials such as water or a map. But sometimes it all works out, despite the naivete.

There's a lot of optimism in the Page of Wands, but not a lot of forethought. Best to say, then, that the Page of Wands is quick to run into battle—doing things impulsively without thought of consequences or benefit.

The career of Jean-Michel Basquiat could be said to have started at the Page of Wands stage. He was a street artist in 1980s New York City first, which meant that, without any thought of what might change in the future, he painted on walls and doors as part of the duo SAMO. When Basquiat later became famous, those doors and walls became insanely valuable. People profited off of his work by dismantling the walls to capture the art. (Banksy is another artist who creates in this way, causing similar problems. People have removed walls in order to possess his art and then sell it for their own gain.)

Basquiat's art matured, so he got out of the Page stage. But his success meant that the art establishment had to take street art seriously in a way it never had before. And street art—owned by no one; often unsigned or signed with a pseudonym—is a very Page of Wands way to create: without personal financial gain, and with the knowledge that the art can be easily destroyed or painted over.

Basquiat also worked with very Wands themes, such as politics and societal critique. As such, he has become hugely influential after his short life, which ended in 1988 from a drug overdose at the age of twenty-seven. He was as much messenger as creator. His presence looms large in hip-hop, poetry, and visual art produced after his death.

The Page of Wands can think more about excitement than

about longevity. But if a person is going to stick around, it is best to have some kind of plan. Balancing that sense of naivete, which can be very helpful for inspiration, with a kind of maturity that allows an artist to keep producing and stay alive is tough. Not everyone manages it. If you want to be the Page, try working spontaneously, without any thought as to how this is all going to end up. But if you want to move past that, you're going to have to look to other cards to see how to grow up a little.

RECOMMENDED MATERIALS

The Notebooks, book by Jean-Michel Basquiat
Exit Through the Gift Shop, documentary film directed by Banksy
"Zine Culture: Brilliance Under the Radar," essay in book
   51 Feminist Essays from the 21st Century by Kirsten Anderberg

PAGE of PENTACLES

·◄─ PAGE OF COINS ─►·

The Page here holds aloft a shining coin. Flowers, trees, and moun-tains can be seen behind him.

The Page of Coins delivers a message to you about the real world, about your body, about work and money. It could be a new under-standing of how these things work. It could also be that these things give you a new sense of pleasure.

Sometimes there is an idea that changes everything. That idea doesn't belong to any one person. A couple different people might have come up with the idea at the same time. But it changes the world. And for generations, people will work with that idea to push it forward and see what else we can figure out.

The idea of evolution was bestowed not only to Charles Darwin but also to his British rival Alfred Russel Wallace. I say "bestowed" because that is how it can seem when a couple different people start to work on the same idea at the same time. Obviously this is something that Darwin toiled over to document and prove. But so did Wallace.

Evolution was a shocking concept. It changed the way that people thought about God, about life, about nature. It wasn't solely Darwin's idea, but that is how we credit it. But this idea became like a gift to humanity. The idea crept into the imaginations of many. Scientists, poets, philosophers, and clergy all took this idea and worked with it, took it apart, and put it back together again in new forms. They took this idea, about the earth, about the body, about the natural world, and changed the way we all think.

So the Page of Coins gives us something that has to be worked with diligently and transformed. It can change shape, find its way into many different genres, and still have an infinite potential for variation.

If you are the Page here, you have an idea that can be used in many different ways. Like how Henry James found endless inspiration in the complicated father-daughter dynamic. Or how American sculptor Louise Bourgeois found herself drawn to spiders again and again in her art. Or, if you're following in the Page's footsteps, you've been tasked with taking someone else's idea and pushing it forward.

Either way, it takes work to put that idea into the world. And the Coins are, in part, the suit of work. So get to it.

RECOMMENDED MATERIALS

The Offering, painting by Saturnino Herran

Wallace, Darwin, and the Origin of Species, book by
    James T. Costa

Darwin: A Life in Poems, book by Ruth Padel

THE KNIGHTS

The Knights are the fire bringers. When a Knight shows up in a reading, it's a mark that it's time to go to war, to relentlessly pursue the thing you desire, or to slay the dragon that is stalking you. It's not just about dutifully marking off items on a to-do list. It is about seeing the task in front of you as a divine mission. The suit of the Knight clues you in as to how to strategize your advance and what kind of attack you'll be making.

The easiest way to understand the Knights is to think about them through the language of battle. A knight requires discipline and devotion. She is strong from years of training, and now all of that practice needs to be put to use. The knights do not choose the war they are fighting, nor did they create the situation they find themselves in. But now that they are here, they will use their loyalty to the cause or to their leader to see them through. The Knight is fearless, but the Knight is also unstable. Young and inexperienced, he sees everything as a war to be waged, even love.

When a creator is living out the archetype of a Knight, he shows bravery and drive. Because she is representing fire, though, if she does not learn how to mature into a more sustainable role, they can easily "burn out." Which is why so many of the Knight archetypes that will follow die young. And there are other downsides to the

THE KNIGHTS

Knight: an inability to see the larger forces at work, an inability to put down his arsenal, a lack of understanding that sometimes peace is a greater show of strength than force.

KNIGHT OF SWORDS

This is the realm of the intellect, so you need to think out your strategy, use your words to get what you want, and be willing to move quickly and adroitly. Outsmart your opponent.

KNIGHT OF CUPS

Love is a battlefield and all that. Here you're fighting for the soul and for the heart, you're trying to woo the maiden. You must be willing to be romantic, idealistic, and emotionally engaged. Don't think, dream.

KNIGHT OF WANDS

Passion, adventure, and excitement are what moves the Knight of Wands. What you're working on has to set your hair on fire and quicken your pulse. Get angry; let that be your fuel.

KNIGHT OF COINS

This is the Knight you take on the Crusades, not to a battle that will be over in a day. He's in it for the long haul. You need to think long-term strategy here.

KNIGHT of SWORDS .

·▸· KNIGHT OF SWORDS ·◂·

An armored knight with a sword in his hand sits on his horse, ready for battle.

The Knight of Swords uses his words to fight his battle. He or she is forthright and dedicated but exists entirely in the present tense. There is no sense of history for the Knight of Swords and no image of what the future might bring. These individuals are dedicated to the task at hand because it is required of them.

When Irmgard Keun found out that her books had been banned by the Nazis, she decided there was only one thing she could do: she sued for lost income.

As one might expect, Germany quickly became an unsafe place for her. It wasn't just her books—sharp satires of ordinary people who allowed the rise of Nazism to happen because they were too busy fixing their hair and going to parties—she basically stood up, waved her arms about, and yelled, "Hey, over here! Come and get me!" Keun fled Germany with her lover Joseph Roth, an Austrian journalist and novelist, but then faked her suicide and sneaked back into the country under an assumed name. After all, this was her country, too. She couldn't just abandon it to the bad guys.

Irmgard Keun is a perfect example of the Knight of Swords archetype. The Knight of Swords is the dragon slayer. She doesn't think about the socioeconomic situation that created the dragon. She doesn't try to reason with the dragon or plan for a dragon-free future. She slays the dragon because *there is a dragon*. It is that simple.

Irmgard Keun wrote against the Nazis because there were Nazis, without much concern for her safety or her future. Osip Mandelstam recited his protest poetry against the brutal Soviet dictator Joseph Stalin in public, knowing that he was inviting danger, but he did it because Stalin was the dragon. He died in a prison camp.

Swords are words and thoughts, and the Knight of Swords knows how to use his words as weapons. It's not simply about saying "No!" or heckling power from the crowd. It's about using your ability to put thoughts and words into action, to sway others, and to encourage dissent. One doesn't simply slay the dragon by waving weapons around and making noises to scare it off. One has to know where to strike and where vulnerability lies, but also how to get others on your side; to get them to see the dragon as a dragon.

That does not mean the Knight of Swords is always able to distinguish the dragon from the not-dragon themselves. Certainly Louis-Ferdinand Céline was a brilliant writer who then used his words to stir up hatred against the Jews in prewar Paris. Many British intellectuals supported Stalinism and wrote propaganda for the regime, not recognizing totalitarianism for what it was.

When working with the energy of the Knight of Swords, you have to be sure that your eyes are clear and your intentions are pure. The brain can play tricks. Logic can lead us down black holes. Which master are you serving? Is that a dragon or a maiden you are slaying with your sword? These are important questions to ask when this card turns up. Be sure you are not plowing your weapon into an innocent's heart.

RECOMMENDED MATERIALS

After Midnight, book by Irmgard Keun

"The Stalin Epigram," poem by Osip Mandelstam

The SCUM Manifesto, radical feminist manifesto by
    Valerie Solanas

KNIGHT of CUPS.

KNIGHT OF CUPS

A knight, dressed in armor, sits on horseback but holds a cup instead of a weapon. The mood is soft, romantic.

The Knight of Cups is the romantic Knight, the Grail Knight. Here the fight is for the heart or for the soul. But love is still a battle for the Knight of Cups. Once it has been won, there is nothing left to do, and he or she loses interest quickly.

In every group of knights, there's always going to be one guy who is more interested in wooing maidens than in fighting wars. That guy would be the Knight of Cups, the romantic soul.

The image of the Knight of Cups immediately brings to mind the search for the Grail, and that is a perfectly good metaphor for how to think about this particular card. In the King Arthur stories, it's the knights who are on a divine mission, who are willing to get lost, who are willing to let their intuition be their guide and stumble upon their sacred prize.

One thinks of someone like Frédéric Chopin, who showed up on the planet already hooked into some sort of divine musical source. He was a child prodigy; music seemed to spill out of him. By seven, he was giving concerts and composing polonaises. He worked constantly, until one day the line between Chopin and the music snapped, and it all went away. He did not live long after that. The music that came before his death was very Knight of Cups. His themes of nostalgia, haunting pieces of regret and love lost, of longing for homes to which one can never return, were of a watery, romantic soul.

Or think of Jeff Buckley, another child prodigy, who began playing guitar at the age of five. His music, with repeated subjects of drowning, mysticism, and the dream world, ran on similar themes. For the Knight of Cups, reaching out is the significant act, not actually grabbing hold. He or she prefers the fog and uncertainty; reality can be a bit too much.

That can tip over into madness or get lost in fantasy if the Knight of Cups is not sufficiently grounded. King Ludwig II of Bavaria referred to himself as the Swan King, and he had grand plans for castles and other structures. He was frustrated, though, by things like the laws of physics. He demanded that the architect of his castle include a rushing river running down a staircase in the castle. When the architect explained this was just not possible, Ludwig became angry and violent. With another building, Ludwig insisted on a pond on the roof. Guests in the bedroom below had to deal with water leaking through the ceiling and dripping down on them throughout the night, scared to complain to the king.

Whatever the inspiration or connection the Knight of Cups carries, if she or he cannot translate that into something that can exist in the real world, it loses its power. That can be a struggle with this card, as what exists in the mind or in the source of inspiration can be more enchanting than what turns up on the page. Persevering through imperfection, surrendering to limitations, can be difficult.

What the Knight of Cups wants is for you to dissolve into fantasy, to take an imaginary being for your lover, to find a muse, to dream of worlds that do not exist yet. To commune with the spirits and build castles in the sky. But then learn how to replicate them on solid ground when you're done.

RECOMMENDED MATERIALS

"Love's Philosophy," poem by Percy Bysshe Shelley

Venus Grotto at Linderhof Palace, designed by King Ludwig II of Bavaria

Nocturne no. 5 in F-sharp Major op. 15 no. 2, musical composition by Frédéric Chopin

Pelléas and Mélisande, opera by Claude Debussy

KNIGHT OF WANDS

An armored knight rides into battle, his horse bucking beneath him. He carries a large wand, used as a staff.

The Knight of Wands might be the most courageous of the Knights, but he or she is also the most arrogant. The Knight of Wands is powerful in short bursts—you would use him to fight in a skirmish, but you would not take him to lay siege to a city. The Knight of Wands is armed with anger, passion, and righteousness. He fights by overwhelming you rather than by any thought-out strategy.

Knight of Wands are double fire: the Knight court card is aligned with fire, and the suit of Wands represents fire. That makes this card an overwhelming inferno of all that fire represents: passion, creativity, desire, and, yes, anger.

It is a rare creator who can use anger to good ends. Virginia

Woolf cautioned against writing in an angry state in *A Room of One's Own*, preferring writing that is calm, cool, and gazing on the action from a distance. And yet without anger in our creative toolbox, we'd have no punk music, no Riot Grrl movement, no David Wojnarowicz.

Part of the difficulty of using anger for creativity is directing it properly. So often there is collateral damage, and the artist is left destroyed as well. Artist Wojnarowicz was living through New York City's AIDS crisis, knowing that he himself had the disease and watching his friends die around him. And he heard the politicians either refusing to discuss the problem or laying blame on the homosexual community, calling their deaths divine retribution. He funneled that frustration and rage into his art and into his book *Close to the Knives: A Memoir of Disintegration*, published in 1991, a year before he died. Wojnarowicz's fury became beautiful, and his anger sang to any number of marginalized and forgotten people who, too, were furious for being abandoned.

There are so many books and top ten lists and magazine articles that will tell you how to control your anger or how to diminish it. Few will say how to use it constructively. The writer, psychologist, and revolutionary Frantz Fanon saw firsthand in Algeria how colonialism and systemic violence wrecked the psyches of the people around him. Fanon, whose own ancestral history came from slavery and who was raised on an island ruled by a Western nation far away, understood the anger that builds when a person is not allowed control of his or her own existence. His 1961 book *The Wretched of the Earth* examined the necessity of violence for the oppressed to overthrow their oppressors, and how anger becomes a source of vitality.

But in every riot, there are those who know what they are fighting for and those whose only mission is to create chaos. They just want to throw bombs; they don't care who or what the target is. There's also the problem with misdirected rage: for example, the artist whose work is cold and calculated but who then beats his wife or rages against his peers. The Knight of Wands asks us to *use* our anger, not suffer from it. The card asks us, What are the underlying systems that are keeping us powerless? Can we find the true source of the situations that fill us with rage? And can we direct that rage creatively and effectively?

If anger is not stifled, it can be a source of inspiration and a way of creating a better world. But when dealing with fire, there is always the risk of it getting out of control. Let it illuminate, let it show you the way, but don't wrap your arms around it. One must keep it from consuming everything it touches.

RECOMMENDED MATERIALS

The Wretched of the Earth, book by Frantz Fanon
Rimbaud in New York, series of photographs by
    David Wojnarowicz
King Kong Theory, book by Virginie Despentes
London Calling, recording by the Clash
"Dead Men Don't Rape," recording by 7 Year Bitch

KNIGHT OF COINS

The Knight of Coins is stationary on his horse, surveying his options. In his hands, he holds a coin; perhaps treasure from a sacked city.

The Knight of Coins is slow to get moving, but once he does, he is unstoppable. He is the Knight of the Crusades—in it for the long haul and also for the plunder. He is grounded, cautious enough to know how not to storm into a predicament that might get him killed, but also dedicated. He wins by outlasting you, by grinding you down slowly.

Ballet was supposed to be prim. Ornate. If anything, it was supposed to transcend the body into something ethereal.

Then Vaslav Nijinsky took the stage as the Faun. He danced onstage with a shawl that reminded him of his love. His tremendous thighs took him high into the air as he leaped; they strained the tights of his costume. It was hard to forget that he was a body. Particularly at the end of the performance, when the shawl dropped to the ground, and the Faun fell on top of it and ground his hips, basically humping the shawl right there in front of the high-society patrons.

It caused a scandal. But the Knight of Coins has a tendency to do that. He is here to teach us something about the human body and about sexuality, and in Western culture, that sort of thing still has the ability to inspire gasps and flushed cheeks.

When earth meets fire, we get the body inflamed. We get sex. We get writers like the nineteenth-century Frenchman Georges Bataille and the twentieth-century German woman Charlotte Roche, separated by three-quarters of a century but still causing scandals with their body- and sex-focused writings. We get painters like Paula Modersohn-Becker, who, instead of showing idealized, no-air-brushing-needed classical versions of the body, painted the female form as it exists. Even when overweight, or sagging, or after giving birth. And we get Nijinsky, screwing a shawl live onstage.

The Knight of Coins wants us to be grounded in our body, it wants us to take it into consideration. Not in the way of dreamy fantasy, all smooth marble and idealized flesh, but the body as it exists. It wants to do away with the taboos we still have about the body, all of the horrors and the areas we won't address. It wants rhythm, it wants Elvis's swinging hips, it wants you to carry around *The Story of O* in your back pocket.

But it is just as easy for the Knight of Coins to get trapped there, striving toward perfection in an unhinged *Black Swan* kind of way. So self-consciously aware of every lump of flesh spilling out in the wrong directions that it can't bear to reveal itself. Attacking the body and all of its faults rather than using that body to attack.

And remember: physical discipline takes time to develop. You can't just sign up for the gym, use the treadmill twice, and then give up because it's too hard or the results aren't coming fast enough. The goal is not to look sexy in a bikini but to have the strength to endure a long battle. A city does not fall in a day. Make sure that you're going to be able to stick it out.

When you draw the Knight of Coins, you need to ask: How is your body engaged with this project? Does how you feel about your own body transmit into the work? Do you take care of your body so that you have the stamina to stay committed to a long-term project, or are you on a Gummi-Bear-and-iced-coffee sugar high? Because the Knight of Coins believes in doing the work, in showing up every day until the job is done—and for that, one needs to keep the body as strong as the mind.

RECOMMENDED MATERIALS

Afternoon of a Faun, ballet choreographed by Vaslav Nijinsky
Sitting Female with One Foot Over Another, painting by
    Paula Modersohn-Becker
Wetlands, book by Charlotte Roche
Black Swan, film directed by Darren Aronofsky

THE QUEENS

The Queens, more than just about anything else, *feel*. They love, they desire, they weep, they laugh. Even when they are thinking about something, they are feeling it, too.

Which is not to say the Queens are passive. They fight and rule and build empires as well as anybody else. But their motivations spring from their emotions. With the Queens, everything they do is intensely personal. So when one of these cards shows up, it is time to examine your own feelings about the project and work from there.

It's also important to remember that the Queens have dignity. They show restraint. They might be working from their feelings, and we all know that feelings can get a little runny-mascara-level messy, but all of that happens behind closed doors. They are not exhibitionists, and they are not indiscreet. They might run around, having affairs, drinking wine from the bottle, and lying on the floor crying, but when they are in front of an audience, they suck it up. They do not make scenes. If you want a scene, you had better look to the Knights.

Part of that is simply because Queens know how to make their emotions be useful to them. When you're at the mercy of your emotional state, then you're crying in public and so on. When you are using that emotional state to power your work, you transform it into creative fuel—into something glorious. Certainly Queen Elizabeth I, who ruled the British Empire from 1542 until her death in 1603, was a human being with all of the mess and disorder that implies, but to her subjects, she was the Virgin Queen. Untouchable, unmovable.

Allow yourself to feel deeply when you're with the Queens. And then find a way to express it through your work.

QUEEN OF SWORDS

Traditionally the Ice Queen or the Virgin Queen; the person who can put her emotions on the shelf in order to be a thoughtful ruler. But don't be mistaken—the emotions are there. They are just a little distant so the Queen can get some work done.

QUEEN OF CUPS

She (or he) does what she does because she cares so much. This is about compassion, care, and love. This Queen puts the needs of others before her own and appears to draw from an infinite stash of empathy.

QUEEN OF WANDS

This is the Queen of Desire. She knows what she wants, and she absolutely knows how to get it. It's more about seduction than triumph, however. The Queen of Wands knows how to draw what she wants to her. She does not chase.

QUEEN OF COINS

A good way to think of the Queen of Coins is as a gardener. Cultivating the things that will pay off down the line, weeding out anything that distracts from her resources, creating boundaries, and remaining committed to her vision.

·•· QUEEN OF SWORDS ·•·

A queen on her throne is looking straight ahead at what lies before her. She holds her sword aloft.

The Queen of Swords uses her wit and intelligence to rule. She would perhaps be Queen Elizabeth I, who maneuvered around her enemies strategically but was also ready to ride into battle.

I always think of the Queen of Swords as a photographer. There is an interest in the subject—maybe even something that can be thought of as love—but the photographer must distance herself from the subject in order to capture it. She puts up this barrier of the camera, and she must set aside her love for a moment to think about shadow, light, framing, and so on. Her love is where things begin as the inspiration, but then the artist, the thinker, the craftsman takes over.

That distance from the love allows the subject to be examined thoroughly. Love is, after all, a foggy state, all moonbeams and crashing waves and delirious swooning. It changes our focus: all of the faults kind of blur out while their virtues are shown in Technicolor. To truly pin down an object of love, one has to remove oneself (a little) from that dreamy state to keep it all from getting mushy and soft.

The photographer Sally Mann created beautiful and loving images of her children. She portrayed them as they were, which included their injuries, their nudity, their half-wild, playful frenzies. In her memoir, *Hold Still*, she remarked that she had to stop being their mother in the moment it took to take each photograph, and become simply an artist instead. Her children were her collaborators, but she had to remove her love for them from the setup in order to take the shot. She couldn't worry about their scraped knees and bloody noses, she couldn't desire to wrap them in blankets to warm them, she couldn't worry how the images of her half-naked five-year-old daughter would be seen by others—she had to put that aside to take the shot. It took, as she wrote, "a sliver of ice" in her heart. Only after the picture had been taken could she return to being their mother.

And that is the role of the Queen of Swords. Many writers have had to distance themselves from their lovers in order to write about them, from Marguerite Duras's hypnotic *The Lover*, to Calvin Trillin's account of his wife's death, *About Alice*. There has to be a sliver of ice to give the Queen a little perspective. To give the love some form.

But it's important to remove the ice, to go back to loving. The Queen of Swords can detach too much. She can wield her sword not toward the art but toward the lover. Dissection is a powerful act, but it should happen on the page or on the film or on the canvas, and not on the living person. It will take a little compartmentalization to get the balance right, but it can be easy for this particular Queen to slide into cruelty.

So use the sword in the right direction and for the right reasons. To examine, not to wound. And know when it's time to put down the sword and reach out with your hands again instead.

RECOMMENDED MATERIALS

The photography of Diane Arbus

The Lover, book by Marguerite Duras

Hold Still, book by Sally Mann

Documenting Science, book of photography by Berenice Abbott

QUEEN of CUPS.

-•- QUEEN OF CUPS -•-

The Queen of Cups sits gazing at the chalice she holds on her lap.

The Queen of Cups is an emotional, compassionate person. She assists in caring for others out of love and concern, not for any material gain. She is a devoted romantic partner, but she sees her family as being her community, her circle of friends. Her love is boundless— sometimes to her detriment.

You know that thing people say: "Get in touch with your feelings"? The Queen of Cups would laugh, hard, if someone told her that. The Queen of Cups isn't just in touch with her feelings, she's swimming in them. At any given moment, she's in danger of being submerged by them. She doesn't have to "check in" with herself or "dig deep" to figure out how she feels about something. All of that is right on the surface for her.

The question is, what can we do with those feelings? Think of the Queen of Cups as a roiling sea. We can use that sea to create electricity and power our cities, or we can dive into it and pull up fish with which to sustain ourselves, or we can flail around in it and drown. The Queen of Cups, at her best, uses her emotions as a resource. She knows where the treasure is buried, and she knows not to wander into dangerous areas. Her emotional map is well documented, even the weirder areas that read "Here Be Monsters."

And so with the Queen of Cups, you see many acts of great compassion. Dian Fossey certainly was a Queen of Cups. Born in 1932 to rather emotionally stunted parents, she befriended animals instead. They became her companions. When she grew up, she chose gorillas as her subject for study, and she went to Africa to observe and write about their culture.

But it wasn't just about watching and reporting for her. Fossey became an active participant in the gorillas' lives. She came to love them. And because of that, she fought to protect them. She assisted in the arrests of poachers, she campaigned for the protection of their habitat, and she became a voice for their interests in the region. She sacrificed her life for their sake, staying involved and active despite many threats to her life. She was eventually murdered for her advocacy work, in 1985.

Because of Fossey's work, however, we know so much more about the mountain gorillas than we would have. And conservation started much sooner. Her love advanced both scholarship and environmental protection.

But for every Dian Fossey, there are many more who are at the mercy of their emotions, or whose love becomes a destructive, rather than creative, force. Men and women who stay in terrible relationships, artists who abandon their work because their spouses don't like it. Certainly someone like Cosima Wagner exemplifies the misguided Queen of Cups. Although a very talented pianist in her own right, she discarded her musical work to assist her husband, famed German composer Richard Wagner, with his.

Love can make us stronger, but it can also make us weaker. The Queen of Cups has no distance from her love, and so it can be easier for her to fall prey to its darker side. Use your love for good.

RECOMMENDED MATERIALS

Gorillas in the Mist, film directed by Michael Apted

Cosima Wagner: The Lady of Bayreuth, book by Oliver Hilmes

The Boating Party, painting by Mary Cassatt

QUEEN OF WANDS

The Queen of Wands sits on her throne, holding her wand like a scepter. She is often accompanied by a pet cat.

The Queen of Wands is a person of passion, but in the mode of receptivity. The Queen does not go out hunting for what she wants, she waits for what she wants to come to her. She is a figure of seduction.

Desire is the key to the Queen of Wands. That is her preferred condition. If she wants something, she draws it into her life. If she wants information, she'd go about getting it like Mata Hari—the exotic-dancer-turned-German-spy, executed by France for espionage during World War I—seducing and performing and crossing borders with ease, playing one government against the other. If she wanted fortune, she would go about it like Coco Chanel, using what she wanted to see in clothing and fashion as a template for how a woman should dress, thereby creating an international empire.

But the greatest model for desire is probably a man: the incomparable Giovanni Giacomo Casanova of eighteenth-century Italy. Certainly he desired women. But Casanova did not stop there. He sought adventure, play, intellectual stimulation. He gambled, he seduced, he was arrested for insulting religion (and, of course, then escaped from jail). Like many of the Queens of Wands, he was a spy, moving from one country to the next. It's not really even because of some overwhelming loyalty to the state that Queens spy; it's because it thrills them to get away with it.

Casanova sums up the Queen of Wands's position quite neatly in his memoirs: "Be the flame and not the moth." In other words, be the figure that excitement, sex, and adventure are drawn to rather than running after it, burning yourself out in the process. If you want something or someone, seduce it. Don't knock it over the head with a rock and drag it back to your cave. Be sophisticated. It's not about competition, it's not about winning. It's about being alluring.

The story of Lilith in mythology is another good example. She was originally made to be Adam's partner, but she found him sexually unfulfilling. Adam wanted Lilith to be submissive, and she did not have time for that. So she left him. They were the first two humans created; it wasn't like she had a lot of choice for sexual partners on the planet. So she consorted with demons instead. They were much more fun and didn't mind that she wanted to be on top.

It's not about taking, it is about *receiving*. A low-end version of the Queen of Wands would decide to pursue a man even if he was married with a family. It's more thrilling for some people to take from others. In fact, they want something only if it belongs to someone else. They feel victorious only if someone else feels defeated.

But Casanova, while he certainly seduced lots of married women, did it not to steal them away from their husbands but to bring them pleasure for the first time. He wanted to adore them; he didn't seek to break up the marriage. What was he going to do with a wife? Knowing what we truly want, rather than what people tell us we want, is a surprisingly complicated task. Be certain what it is that you want—and then draw it to you. The Queen of Wands is magnetic in her desire.

RECOMMENDED MATERIALS

The Story of My Life, book by Giovanni Giacomo Casanova
Signed, Mata Hari, book by Yannick Murphy
"Lobster dress," designed by Elsa Schiaparelli

QUEEN of PENTACLES

◦—◦ QUEEN OF COINS ◦—◦

The throne of the Queen of Coins is situated in a field or garden. She sits holding a coin in her hands.

The Queen of Coins is a queen of fertility and fecundity. She is practical and thrifty. She knows how to make much with very little, the kind of person who can create a feast out of whatever is in the pantry. As such, this queen is never in a state of want.

Let's continue with the gardening metaphor for the Queen of Coins because it really is useful. With a garden, you are not thinking about right now, you are looking into the future. You're planting seeds with the expectation that they'll eventually turn into something useful and beautiful. You're on your knees weeding and watering and protecting your plants from insects and snails every day. You're planning for the next season, and the season after that, as you make decisions about herbicides versus weeding, pesticides versus natural remedies. And what do you get for all of your trouble? Bounty.

The Queen of Coins is all about diligence. You do the small work because you know it can turn into something magnificent and big. You get your hands dirty because you know that is how you make something beautiful. You use a lot of different elements because the sum is greater than the parts.

She would be as focused on the environment as she would be focused on her own ambitions. People who embody the Queen of Coins often start up organizations or companies that allow them to collaborate with other like-minded artists and help nurture a larger audience. Certainly the choreographer and dancer Martha Graham could have been a solo artist for other people's dance companies. There is less responsibility and less pressure that way. But she started her own company, to have more control and also to create a working environment that suited her best. She could choose who she wanted to work with and how her work was presented.

But a grander example would be Sergey Diaghilev, who created the dance company Ballets Russes in the early twentieth century. He didn't only work with dancers: Diaghilev also commissioned new music from cutting-edge composers such as Igor Stravinsky and Claude Debussy, he asked fashion designers like Coco Chanel to create costumes, he commissioned art for backdrops by Pablo Picasso and the Russian painter Léon Bakst. He created a full revolution in art and performance.

His dancers, from Nijinsky to Anna Pavlova, became superstars, as did many of the composers and artists with whom he collaborated. He knew how to create an environment where everyone could create and contribute his or her best work. For Diaghilev, it wasn't about money, it was about art. Every dollar he earned, if not more, was invested back into the company. Diaghilev had no real artistic talent of his own, so he nurtured it in others.

Just remember to take care of yourself while you're taking care of everyone else. Turn that nurturing energy inward every once in a while. And don't get so focused on the mundane routine that you forget to enjoy the fruits of your labors. The Queen of Coins can be a little too stuck in the mud sometimes; it's important that she be able to get off her feet every now and then.

RECOMMENDED MATERIALS

Diaghilev and the Ballets Russes, 1909–1929, book by
Jane Pritchard
The Firebird, ballet by Igor Stravinsky
Martha Graham: Dance on Film, DVD directed by Nathan Kroll

THE KINGS

The Kings might as well be renamed the Philosophers, at least for our purposes. Belonging to the quality of air, the Kings represent thought, detachment, reason. In order to gain perspective and truly understand something, you have to get far enough away from it—take an aerial view—so that you can see it in its entirety. That is what the King is able to do. He removes himself from the situation so that he can assess it dispassionately.

Like all of the other court cards, the Kings are more about behavior and character than they are about gender. The King does not necessarily represent a man. Instead, it is the quality of thought that distinguishes the King.

So when a King appears, it is time to get philosophical. All of your messy (wonderful) feelings? Put them to the side. Your hopes and desires? The same. It is time to think through your problem in a cool, reasoned manner, and the suit of the King that appears will show you how and where to do this. The King differs from something like Justice, however, by his (or her) methods. It is not about distancing oneself in order to see what is fair. It is about distancing oneself to see the truth.

To be the King, one must first be wise, and so these cards might be calling you to add to your reading list. You cannot simply rely on common sense or skimming a *New Yorker* article to save you here. In order to fully understand something, one must examine it from every angle and consider different viewpoints. This is about pursuing wisdom.

KING OF SWORDS

The embodiment of logic himself, the King of Swords wants you to examine your situation mathematically. Equations and formulas are most comfortable for our King, and the scientific method is his muse.

KING OF CUPS

This King might be a lover, but he also understands the power of attachment, the biological and hormonal responses of love, and the dimensions of the soul. He has a heart and knows how to love, but the logic of his love makes it all the more powerful.

KING OF WANDS

Can one philosophize fury? Passion? Anger? The King of Wands examines everything that sets him aflame and will find its psychological source. This understanding makes his passion sustainable, keeping him from burning out.

KING OF COINS

Here we find the Stoics, the economists, and the pragmatists. Also the Communists and radicals. It's money and work that find their philosophical centers here, as well as the body and the earth.

KING OF SWORDS

A king on his throne, his sword used not as a weapon but more as a symbol of his power.

The King of Swords is an intellectual. He is able to control his thoughts and use logic and reason to good ends. He might be a little disconnected from his emotions, however.

All of the great breakthroughs of science and logic occur because the scientist is able to remove himself from the accepted knowledge of the day and see other possibilities. When a person is immersed in the common way of thinking, when he simply accepts conventional wisdom rather than look for his own method of proving or disproving it, they can fall into fallacies. Think of all of the astronomers who for centuries "proved" that the Earth was the center of the solar system. By looking only for evidence to shore up this belief, they were easily able to ignore everything that showed otherwise.

And so the great minds, from astronomer Johannes Kepler to physicist Albert Einstein, were able to step aside from the current mode of thinking and make great leaps forward in knowledge. That is one of the tasks of the King of Swords: to ask if you've accepted something as true simply because everyone else has, and then discover new and novel ways of approaching problems.

From the nineteenth century and through two world wars, Vienna, Austria, was a meeting place for great minds who were willing and capable of dismantling common knowledge and replacing it with bold, world-changing theories. Two who got their starts there were Ludwig Boltzmann and Kurt Gödel. Boltzmann's work in thermodynamics predicted the behavior of atoms and molecules and advanced the field of physics, while Gödel's theorems on the incompleteness of mathematics influenced widely the fields of philosophy, mathematics, and physics. It was the interaction, conversation, and writing that allowed the Viennese to flourish the way they did—all three very much Swords activities.

The King of Swords wants conversation to think through his ideas and also to allow others to influence him. He (or she) wants to write, to communicate, to contemplate. He wants to argue, but only through logic, never out of anger or passion. He wants to read and to know.

What both Boltzmann and Gödel did was to insert uncertainty into certainty; chaos into form. And both accomplished this by standing back from what was accepted knowledge at the time— that the world was knowable and understandable, that it functioned by a set of never-changing rules—and seeing the cracks.

But there are downsides to the King of Swords, and both men would fall prey to them. Logic, taken too far, can begin to eat itself, leading to depression, anxiety, and paranoia. When thoughts are allowed to run amok, they can start to destroy the mind from which they sprung. Boltzmann ended his life through suicide. Gödel fell into a paranoia so deep that he became convinced he was being poisoned by unknown enemies; he refused to eat until he finally starved to death.

It's important to make sure your detachment is serving you and not isolating you. It's important to allow your ideas to come into contact with others' ideas, to make sure they stand up to testing. But mostly it's important to refine your intellect. The King of Swords is brilliant, and that is something to aspire to.

RECOMMENDED MATERIALS

Incompleteness: The Proof and Paradox of Kurt Gödel, book by
    Rebecca Goldstein
Ludwig Boltzmann: Man, Physicist, Philosopher, book by
    Englebert Broda
On the Revolution of Heavenly Spheres, book by
    Nicolaus Copernicus

KING of CUPS.

·⊷· KING OF CUPS ·⊷·

The King of Cups is seated and is holding a cup close to his chest. He does not look into it, but gazes outward. It is not clear if he is offering you the cup or is keeping it for himself.

The King of Cups is traditionally seen as the romantic figure—more committed and stable than the Knight; less wishy-washy than the Queen. But the King is also thoughtful and concerned about others, or a spiritual figure.

When it comes to the matters of the heart, the King of Cups prefers to take an intellectual approach. He can dissect the various methods of love, its biological and its emotional components, and the historical and sociological pressures on a couple to marry. He would watch a romantic comedy and understand how it relates to myths such as Psyche and Eros, Tristan and Isolde, and he would have something to say on how these movies give their viewers unrealistic expectations for emotional connection. He will also have read a lot of Freud.

None of this should impact the King of Cups's ability to feel and to love, however. The understanding, if anything, adds depth to his emotions. The King does not reach this level of knowledge in order to scheme. He is not trying to game anyone or learn bogus seduction techniques. He simply wants to understand his own heart in order to survive its pangs and know what to do with it.

At the time that Harry Harlow was studying psychology in the 1920s, there was a strange atmosphere in the scientific community. Male doctors were instructing new mothers not to touch their babies. Too much touch and too much comfort would make a baby soft and dependent as he or she grew older, they contended. Better to let the infant learn self-sufficiency, cry out his problems, and figure out what to do on her own. It would lead to strong, intelligent men and women.

Harlow knew this was nonsense, and he decided to prove it. He would separate baby monkeys from their mothers and put them in cages to see how they reacted. He would create fake monkey mothers out of cloth and wire—the cloth ones provided no food, while those fashioned from wire did—and see which ones the babies preferred. Even when hungry, they would cling to the soft cloth mother. Babies without any touch at all simply didn't thrive. Many became violent, anxious, and began to hurt themselves. Babies need touch and love, he determined—as much, if not more so, than they need food.

Harlow's studies revolutionized our understanding of love and the human need for it. Periodically we decide that the need for love must be weakness, and then someone—a King of Cups—goes about proving it's essential for human life.

Like all the Kings, the risk is overabstraction. That by studying love and emotions they run the risk of separating themselves from it. Or, understanding the darker side of love so well, they can't let themselves trust ever again. Harlow himself was a terrible husband, or so said his first wife Clara Mears. Cold and distant, showing more concern and attention to his monkeys than to his own family. But in general, the King of Cups can recite Shakespeare's sonnets, explain the science of attachment, quote studies on the evolutionary advantages of love, and yet refuse to give himself over to the actual experience of it.

But the King of Cups has a tremendous capacity for love and emotional connection, if he is willing to accept that the strangest aspects of love cannot be dissected logically. Love is as mysterious as the soul, and people have been trying to figure out that thing for centuries without much luck. The brain will take you only so far into love; the rest of the way has to be lit with uncertainty.

RECOMMENDED MATERIALS

The Seven Storey Mountain, book by Thomas Merton
*Mothers and Others: The Evolutionary Origins of Mutual
    Understanding*, book by Sarah Blaffer Hrdy
Love at Goon Park: Harry Harlow and the Science of Affection,
    book by Deborah Blum

·•· KING OF WANDS ·•·

The King of Wands is dressed boldly, in robes the colors of flame. He sits on the edge of his seat, incapable of staying in repose.

The King of Wands is nothing if not charismatic. His energy and his enthusiasm are infectious. He (or she) is a creative thinker, quick on his feet, and always ready for a new adventure. This King always needs a new task to complete, or he will start to crack. He can see a project through to completion and has a command over his skills and talents.

Emma Goldman, an American political activist during the late nineteenth and early twentieth centuries, was trouble, but then, the King of Wands usually is. When one starts thinking about all of that fiery energy—sex, revolution, ecstasy, passion, creativity, rage—authorities have, historically, not responded well. Goldman was thrown in jail, slandered, censored, harassed, and, finally, the

275

US government had her deported. All because she wanted to talk publicly about issues that made the people in power uncomfortable.

The combination of air and fire is a particularly powerful one. Oxygen sustains the flame, and wind can spread it far and wide. Too much air—like blowing out a candle—and the fire is snuffed out; not enough and the same happens. But when the mix is right, you don't just get a cozy little campfire. You can burn down a whole forest.

So the Kings of Wands have been revolutionaries. Like Maud Gonne, traveling around Ireland during the years when Charles Parnell fought for Home Rule in the late nineteenth century, inciting the people to resist the British occupiers. Or like Leon Trotsky, fighting against the totalitarianism of Russian leader Joseph Stalin and founding the Red Army, before his eventual assassination. Or Rosa Luxemburg, the philosopher who fought against the rise of Nazism in Germany and was such a threat that she was assassinated.

There has to be an intellectual heft behind all of this anger and calls for change, otherwise you risk becoming just a terrorist or a murderer. Like the Red Army Faction in Germany, which formed to fight the failed denazification of the post–World War II government and to bring about a fairer and more just social system, but then just ended up killing without much thought or strategy. Many groups that begin with good intentions end up committing the same kinds of crimes and atrocities that they said they wanted to fight to begin with. The rage takes over and devours all the oxygen in the room.

But truly effective revolutionaries—like Emma Goldman, who

raised consciousness about feminism, the evils of rapacious capital-ism, and sexual freedom; or Angela Davis, who has fought against the American prison system as well as racism and sexism—are able to keep their rage in check through their intellect. They use the tools of the King, such as thought and the pen and speech, to spread the word.

With this card, it's not enough to feel rage or excitement. You must understand what lies beneath those feelings. You must study what you can do to change the situation that makes you angry or to nurture an environment that stimulates you. It's a study of impulses—those urges we fear we cannot control—to see where they come from and also the consequences of acting on them. And then using your charisma and your wit to spark those feelings and those thoughts in others.

RECOMMENDED MATERIALS

Let the Fire Burn, documentary film directed by Jason Osder
Living My Life, book by Emma Goldman
Cesar Chavez: History Is Made One Step at a Time, film directed
  by Diego Luna

KING of PENTACLES.

KING OF COINS

The King of Coins rests easily on his throne, a coin resting under his hand. He is surrounded by the foods of the harvest: grain, grapes, fruit.

The King of Coins knows how to invest in something, whether that be a business, a financial opportunity, or in his own education or training. He is steady enough to see through tumult without wavering in his dedication. He is practical enough not to chase fantasies. The King of Coins knows what he values, and he is willing to work hard to attain those things.

Here the duty of the King is to look at what *is*—not what could be or some longed-for fantasy. What is actually there, in front of you, existing in the real world. Only then can the King figure out what to do with it and how to turn it into something better.

The King of Coins is not a day trader, turning money into an airy abstraction—a few numbers on a digital file and never turned into cash or gold. The King of Coins is not a man who runs off to expand his empire while his homeland crumbles from neglect. The King of Coins is not the farmer who keeps poisoning the land and the water with napalm-strong pesticides and herbicides, with no regard for the consequences. The King of Coins is a pragmatist above all else. He or she works and lives in the real world.

We tend to remember the terrible emperors the best: Ivan the Terrible, Nero, Caligula, Napoléon I, Kaiser Wilhelm II. Men and women who served during times of quiet prosperity, whose citizens were stable and well cared for, whose countries flourished rather than spat out chaos, those all tend to blur together. It's depravity that is exciting. It's insanity that is memorable.

The stable emperors of Rome were so few that they made a list of the "Five Good Emperors," with the rest being mostly murderers, nut jobs, and sociopaths. Marcus Aurelius, who ruled Rome in the second century AD, was its last good emperor. He wasn't just a ruler, he was a Stoic philosopher. The Stoics believed that a person could find stability—a very Coin-ish virtue—if he or she employed reason. That reason could keep the person from wandering too far into his or her own fears or drifting off into fantasy.

In his writings *Meditations*, Marcus Aurelius demanded his readers know themselves, interrogate themselves fully so that they could see their own capacities and limitations. Only then, he suggested, could we achieve our greatest potential.

Like all Coin energy, too much of it can plunge one into depression. With too much reality and not enough hope or frivolity, the weight of it all can press down. It's good to acknowledge your limitations. It's less helpful to be so realistic about your abilities and powers that you foresee only disappointment. Too much reality can make it difficult to get out of bed.

But at his best, the King of Coins understands value, beginning with the value of money—not in terms of hoarding it but in what it can be exchanged for and how it can assist others. The value of time, and the limited amount we are able to do with our lives. The value of work, and how it can turn us into better people. The King of Coins wants to contribute; wants to see things grow and develop. But before any of that, he has to learn how to survey the lay of the land.

RECOMMENDED MATERIALS

Meditations, book of writings by Marcus Aurelius

The Philosophy of Money, book by Georg Simmel and edited by David Frisby

Monoculture: How One Story Is Changing Everything, book by F. S. Michaels

THE SPREADS

Now that we've familiarized ourselves with the cards themselves, and now that we know how to construct a reading, it's time to learn about the spreads.

Spreads are merely templates: ways of arranging the cards to answer your question. You decide in advance which card will stand in for which part of your answer, either because you are using an already established spread or because you are designing your own. For example, one card might represent you, the person asking the question. Another card will represent the direction you should be taking to improve your situation, or maybe the role that another person will be playing.

The spreads help us construct the story we are looking to tell. We create characters and plot, beginnings and conclusions. We use them to put our thoughts and our stories in order. Without knowing what each card is supposed to stand for, the cards are just lying there chaotically and it's hard to determine their meaning. Am I the Queen of Wands? Or is that someone else? Am I moving toward the Five of Cups or away from it? The spreads form the narrative of the story.

There are a few classic tarot card spreads. There is the Celtic Cross, which is the standard reading that is suitable for almost all queries. If you're familiar with the tarot at all, this is the reading you probably know. There's the cross in the center, and then a tower running alongside. There are cards that represent your current influences, who you are in this quandary, and what the outcome is likely to be.

It's a spread that has been used for a very long time, although, as with many things tarot-related, its exact origins have been debated and are ultimately unknown.

But it's also possible to create your own spread if you have a situation that the Celtic Cross does not cover. While I find the Celtic Cross extremely helpful for personal issues, it is less useful for creative issues, simply because it's not built for that kind of story.

I decided, then, to design some spreads for very specific issues involving creativity. Here I'm including a few that I've developed in order to assist with creative problems, both my own and those of my clients. The spreads cover everything from finding inspiration, to structuring a project, to figuring out how to present that project to the world. All of my spreads are quick and direct, they use a minimal number of cards, and each placement is defined clearly to provide maximum clarity. These are very practical spreads for practical concerns. They can be drawn and interpreted rather quickly, so that you can see easily what it is you need to do and then get back to work and do them.

But I want to encourage you to improvise. Nothing below is a science. I developed the spreads through trial and error: by reading for myself and figuring out what worked for me, and also by reading for my clients and listening to what they needed. But, of course, what you need might be different, so feel free to reorder, add or subtract cards from a spread, and so on. Consider these to be suggestions rather than strict rules for how to read for yourself about a creative issue. If you do improvise, remember to mark out in advance what each card in each placement is made to represent. It won't help you to try to rearrange the cards into a "happier" order. The point of using the tarot is to find insight, not simply to reassure ourselves that all is going to end well.

There's also one of my favorite methods of reading, which could not really be called a spread: ask a question, pull one card. Let that card be the answer. Ask another question, pull one card. As in:

"Why am I having trouble with this painting?"

Answer: Four of Coins—trying too hard to control the results.

"How can I fix this?"

Answer: Seven of Cups—be more dreamy, more imaginative, looser.

The cards can be remarkably direct when they want to be. So remember: there is no right way or wrong way to read the cards. If you want to stick with the Celtic Cross, you can easily find guides online on how to interpret that spread. If you want to develop your own spreads, absolutely do so. The cards are merely a tool; you get out of them the work you put in.

CREATIVITY SPREADS

1. Finding Inspiration

Three-card reading. Use Finding Inspiration when you are between projects and feeling uninspired. It can be used to find new avenues worth exploring, can guide you toward parts of your own history that require excavation. Let this reading be your muse.

2. The Creative Block

Seven-card reading. *If you have stalled out on a project, or your way forward seems unclear, the Creative Block is a powerful tool for removing obstacles and getting back on track. It will show you what is in your way and which of your skills and hidden talents you need to deploy. In addition, it will give you a sense of what your next step should be.*

3. Creating Structure

Variable number of cards required. *When you feel your project is too baggy or the right way to order your project evades you, the Creating Structure reading can help. It will help you find the core narrative or ideas of your project, and then place those ideas or that story in the proper order for the best impact.*

4. Checking Your Direction

Eight-card reading. *At the midpoint of a project, we can begin to doubt ourselves and some of the decisions we've made. Checking Your Direction is a good way to bring your project back into alignment, to make sure that the foundations are secure and that your intentions at the beginning are still complementary to the intentions now.*

5. Bringing Your Project into the World

Six-card reading. *Once your project is finished, Bringing Your Project into the World will help you figure out what should be done with it. How should it be presented? Will an outside person be able to assist you? The spread tells you how to define your project, who its audience might be, and how to get it in front of that audience.*

FINDING INSPIRATION

First card: Head
Second card: Heart
Third card: Body

We'll start with an easy reading: a simple three-card draw. We all go through stages when nothing inspires us, when our music collection is boring, none of our books looks appealing, everything you see in the galleries seems like a waste of everyone's efforts. We can also just get into ruts, always going to the same genre or the same type of work for inspiration when we should be branching out. This is a quick reading that can help reinspire you.

The first card we draw here tells us what we should be feeding our brains. What should we be using to refine our intellect? What information are we missing? What do we need to understand before we can move forward?

Too often we rely on our own experiences and emotions in order to fuel our creative work. There's nothing wrong with looking inward, as long as you remember to look outward sometimes, too. If you pull a Minor Arcana card here, the suit will tell you which genre you should look to. A Cups card might indicate that you should fill up on love stories. Swords, and maybe you should be brushing up on your mathematics. A court card might mean that you should troll through the biography section of your bookstore, to find a new muse. Either way, this is about the intellect. It's about sharpening your mind on someone else's stone.

The second card is more about emotion. What will move us?

Which part of your own romantic or family history should you be reexamining?

While the first card tells us where to look outside of ourselves, the heart card is inward-facing. A dark card here, like the Three of Swords or perhaps the Tower, would ask you to examine more chaotic chapters of your own history; maybe darker regions you're reluctant to go. But this can also be a film or a book, albeit one that has a personal connection to your own story.

The third card is for our bodies. It's a card of pleasure, of movement, of discipline. Do you need action or rest? How have you been treating yourself lately?

It's not just our reading habits that can fall into a bland routine; the things we do to and with our bodies can, too. And it affects the way we think and the way we perform. It might be time for a new workout or a new diet. You might be starving your body of pleasure as you toil away into the wee hours. Or maybe you've been self-indulgent and need a little discipline. It could also be that the way you treat your body—with neglect or with shame—is connected in some way to a creative work and needs to be explored. The Devil here might show that you've been handling yourself recklessly, while a Cups card might mean that you should dunk yourself in bodies of water.

How these cards interact with one another will be interesting. If you have swords as your second card, perhaps you've been too reliant on emotion in the past and need to shore up your intellect for a while. If you pull one of the darker cards for the head, you might want to start thinking of researching the philosophy of despair or the biography of a self-destructive artist. And don't be too literal: use the imagery to guide you as much as the definition of the card.

If you see the Five of Wands in the Body position, maybe you need to hit something to release anger.

Also, how you respond to the cards will have a lot to do with which part of your self does the heavy lifting in your creativity. A dancer will be much more aware of how she treats her body, after all, than a writer on a tight deadline. And someone who works directly from the heart might forget to bring logic, history, or thoughtfulness into the process sometimes.

SAMPLE READING

Head: Six of Cups
Heart: Wheel of Fortune
Body: Queen of Coins

If there is a theme to this particular reading, it is the theme of the soul mate.

The Six of Cups is often referred to as the soul mate card, someone with whom you have an innocent, childlike attachment, or the person you just met whom it feels like you've known forever. The Wheel of Fortune at the position of the heart is the big, fated love. And the Queen of Coins is the dedicated, committed partner. All of that adds up to the soul mate as the inspirational source.

You don't have to have a soul mate right now to let the idea inspire you. Intellectually, there are many ways you can go. You can read about the science of attraction, why the smell of one person drives us wild and why another repulses us, how we form our romantic template in childhood. You can read about attachment theory, the physiological basis of love, the history of marriage. This is about expanding the idea further than just your own experiences, to widen the scope of your work.

At the heart, daydream about your ideal, and how that person differs from the men or women in your own romantic history. Remember the moments when meeting someone where it felt fated? Where it felt like the gods moved you around on the earth like it was a chessboard to crash you into this exact person at this exact time? Gorge on the great romantic myths, from Tristan and Isolde to Eros and Psyche. Or the historical love stories where a great romance started a war—or at least diplomatic incidents, like the Trojan War or the life of Cleopatra.

And at the level of the Body, the Queen of Coins is essentially Demeter, the Greek goddess of fertility. It is the muddy, erotic, sex, champagne, and really-good-cheese card. If you don't have a suitor, then by God, seduce yourself. Treat yourself the way you want someone else to treat you. Indulge. Get your hands in the dirt, send yourself flowers, buy yourself fine lingerie without concern about whether anyone else will see it, stay in the bath way past any reasonable amount of time, and, you know . . . take a little time for yourself before bed. If you do have a partner right now, lavish him or her with all of this attention and then demand it for yourself.

Fated love and the soul mate have inspired great works throughout time. Now it's time to inspire yours.

THE CREATIVE BLOCK

First card: You
Second card: Your project

Third and fourth cards: Your obstacles
Fifth card: Your tool to overcome
Sixth card: Next step
Seventh card: Final outcome

We all know this feeling: that there is something standing in the way of what we are trying to accomplish. We're here, the end result is all the way over there, and in between stands this big wall we can't figure out a way around. This is a spread for identifying those obstacles and determining how to overcome them.

The first card represents you as the creator of this project. Which part of you is in charge of the project, which part of you this project came out of. This is helpful to establish because it tells you what your motivations were for taking on this project, as well as what kind of energy and how much you want to invest in it.

The second card is more about what the project needs rather than what you need, and it's important to notice if cards one and two are in conflict. Is one card Wands and the other Coins? That's going to be more difficult to reconcile than if the cards are in harmony. But you can also look at this card (the one representing the project) as a kind of gift. It represents what the project is trying to give you or show you. The project is trying to draw something out of you, and only by accepting that gift can you make progress on the work.

We draw two cards for the obstacles because rarely is it just one thing going wrong. You can pull wonderful cards here, but they can still be bad news. The World is good news just about anywhere else, but as an obstacle, it can ask, "Are you unfocused? Or are you so excited about the prospect of having a finished product that you find it difficult to sit down and do the actual work?" Again, the combination of these two cards tells you more than either card individually.

Sometimes the cards representing the obstacles will be obvious immediately: "Oh, Five of Coins—that's because I feel like I'm out on my own doing this without any support. Got it." Other times, you're going to have to do some digging to figure out what it means. Does the card represent something about yourself that is blocking you, like that nagging voice that always tells us we aren't good enough? Is someone in your life blocking you? Or do the cards represent a wrong choice in your approach?

Justice here could indicate that we're being too detached and logical in our approach. Or it could mean that legal issues involving our project—perhaps copyright permissions or a publishing contract—need to be sorted out. Only you, who knows the exact circumstances of your life, will understand how to properly interpret the cards.

The tool that overcomes the obstacles is a skill we have that needs to be brought into use. Here the suit will tell us much if the card is part of the Minor Arcana. Cups are your intuitive side, Coins your ability to work, Swords your logical self, and Wands your excitement and passion. If it's Major Arcana, it's an archetype that we need to put into play. For example, the Hermit would indicate that we know deep down what we're doing; we just need to listen to our own wisdom. We need to shut out external voices long enough to hear the answer.

What comes next shows us how the tool works and how the obstacles are overcome. Now that we know what our tool is, how do we wield it? Is the next step going to be difficult—as in, do we need to start over entirely? Or is it going to require just some rearranging of our time and process?

The final outcome card then indicates how this all turns out. If this is a long-term project—a four-volume biography or a ten-year course of study—the card would indicate better how this phase of the project ends, rather than the project as a whole.

It is important, however, not to freak out if the final outcome card looks tough, like the Tower or the Ten of Swords—something that would seem to indicate failure. Look, failure is part of the creative process. No one wants to hear that, but it's true. Great writers have burned manuscripts they'd worked on for years, great painters have hacked apart canvases they didn't like. No one really wants to keep going on a project if he suspects it's all going to be a waste of time. However, many times it's not the outcome that's important but the lessons learned along the way. And just because a project doesn't end in publication or worldwide success, that doesn't mean it wasn't worth doing. And hey, we've all seen Oscar-winning movies and read Pulitzer-winning books and thought, *This is terrible! This is a failure.*

But also, the cards are not precise. They do not outline the exact circumstances of how things turn out. There is no Your Agent Rejects Your Manuscript card, after all. The final outcome card does not predict the future, it tells you what the end of this process is *likely* to look like or feel like. It's not easy to detach emotionally from the Tower for a final outcome, but just remember that you have no idea what form the Tower is going to take. It'll be a shake-up, but it can play out a dozen different ways. And even if a project is put into a drawer eventually, the things you learn during the creative process can be incorporated in future work.

SAMPLE READING

You: The High Priestess
Your Project: The Emperor
Obstacles: Strength and Four of Swords
Tool to Overcome Obstacles: The Hanged Man
Next Step: Ten of Swords
Final Outcome: The Empress

Our creator here is the High Priestess, which is a strong card to pull to represent yourself. The High Priestess is wise, learned, knowledgeable. She's mysterious and potent. But she does have a few qualities that can make it hard for her to get to work, and that is reflected in the cards to come.

The High Priestess can be so focused on research, on gathering new information and following her curiosity, that it can be hard to move her from the library to the desk. She might never feel totally prepared to perform—to put her knowledge to use. She's more comfortable in the shadows than she is up onstage, and "research" is a wonderful procrastination tool. There's *always* more to learn.

The project, though, wants to be the Emperor. Something forceful and dynamic. He's a very right-angles-and-four-corners kind of guy, and all of those sharp edges might be too harsh for the High Priestess. To get from her to him requires some real work and a willingness to get dirty.

The Emperor, above all, requires discipline. A project represented by the Emperor would be something that is strongly structured and very orderly. It's the kind of thing you would want to set a schedule to complete; you would want to know where it's going to end before you begin. It requires blueprints.

And so we have two obstacles that echo each other: Strength and the Four of Swords. Both are cards of repose. Strength wants the lion (or the project or the inspiration) to come to her, so she waits patiently for it. The Four of Swords is taking a nap. And these cards together suggest someone who is wandering around her apartment, maybe scrubbing out her bathtub, maybe flipping through art books, waiting for inspiration to strike. But the Emperor requires you to show up for the work, whether you want to or not. These cards of sitting around, being vigilant but still procrastinating, are in line with the High Priestess's desires, which is to never actually get around to *doing* the work but, instead, to always be *preparing* to do the work.

We need to use the Hanged Man to figure out a new way. The Hanged Man is also a card of repose, but he's more active. He realizes that all of this time of sitting back, waiting and learning, was supposed to be about action. You're supposed to get something useful out of it. So the Hanged Man asks this creator to think about what he or she has learned and how to really put it to use. The Hanged Man does come down from his tree eventually. He was up there to invent the alphabet, remember? And that's not just so that he could keep it inside his brain as a secret. It's to share, to help all of mankind with it.

The next step is a bit gruesome: it's the Ten of Swords. The card of surrender. You're not going to like it, but you have to do it anyway. It is the card of resigning yourself to circumstances. You might not like having to work with a tight schedule, or work with an outline, or actually working at all! But it must be done. And so you resign yourself to it.

The final outcome here is the Empress. She gets along with the High Priestess much better than the Emperor, and in a sense, the Empress is the bridge between the two. She's learned, but she's active. She's orderly, but she's creative. It's finding the middle ground between these two figures who don't really get along, and finding creative fertility from that.

CREATING STRUCTURE

This is a good reading to do when things start to get a little out of hand. It can help you rein in an overstuffed project that has too many ideas, or find an order for disparate parts that resist coming together easily.

This is not a spread with a set number of cards or arrangement, because each project will be structured differently. It is a bit more free-form, but still incredibly useful. It helps if you are a little more adept with the deck; if you know the cards well enough that you don't have to keep checking in with the manual. It just helps to be somewhat looser and less literal with the cards for this one.

Look at the project you are creating, or wish to create, and break it into sections. If it's a book, it might make sense to break it into chapters. If it's a collection of artwork, each individual piece can serve as a section. Or you can pick the major parts—like the major points of the narrative arc—or four groupings of material. However you want to work is fine.

Count up how many sections there are, and then draw the same number of cards. Instead of letting the luck of the draw determine which card goes with each section, study the cards carefully and see which one makes the most sense for each section. Assign that card to that section.

Now arrange the cards in the order that would make sense to tell a story. Naturally an Ace would come at the beginning. A card like the Empress or a Knight could represent a character who needs to be introduced. And a Ten or something like the World would make a suitable ending.

Use the story of those cards to reorder your project. For example, I write mostly essays, and when I'm collecting them, it can be difficult to figure out how to order them. It doesn't always make sense to put them in chronological order. So I can group the essays by theme, designate a card to represent each theme, and then use the story of the card to create an arc that had eluded me when looking only at the essays themselves.

Assigning a card to a fragment of the whole also helps you see the essence of that fragment: its core meaning. Is it excessive, and thus fogging up the essential truth? Assigning a card can also help you pare down a bloated fragment to its essence, or figure out how to frame it so that its true nature is showcased better.

SAMPLE READING

I'll use a reading I drew for myself. I selected some essays that I wanted to collect, and divided them into five sections. I drew five cards: Six of Cups, Five of Coins, Three of Coins, Seven of Coins, and the Nine of Coins.

I assigned one card per section. My essays about love? The Six of Cups. I gave the Five of Coins to my essays about poverty and political action. And so on. The Seven of Coins did not line up perfectly with my more humorous essays, but as that card often indicates a pause, I thought it could represent a pause for the reader: a bit of lightness after dealing with some of the darker material.

Looking at just the cards, an order seemed obvious, and that was the numerical order. We start with the Three of Coins, which does indicate the beginning of a large project, and move toward the Nine of Coins, which is achievement. We start off trying to build something new with the Three of Coins, we suffer a setback with the Five of Coins, we recover with the help of the love of the Six of Cups, we patiently endure the work of the Seven of Coins, and then with the Nine of Coins, we achieve completion. Drawing all Coins, save one, was a surprise, and yet it helped me see that the essays *were* cohesive—nothing startled me as being obviously out of place. And if you draw mostly cards of the same suit or the same number but with the Devil thrown in the mix, seemingly out of nowhere, it might be helpful to see if that section should be there at all.

Going back to the original material, I decided to keep the order the cards suggested, although I switched the positions of the Five and the Six. The section I assigned to the Five seemed like the heart of the book, and so it made sense that it would come in the middle. Otherwise, it gave the essays a neat arc.

CHECKING YOUR DIRECTION

First card: You at the beginning of the project
Second card: The project when you began
Third card: Transition

Fourth card: You now
Fifth card: The project now
Sixth card: Transition
Seventh card: You at the end of the project
Eighth card: Project concluded

Sometimes it takes us awhile to finish a project, and when that happens, our intentions, our ideas, our desires change along the way. That can make us start to doubt our direction—or at least wonder how much of our early-stage work is going to have to be rethought or reworked to bring it into alignment.

That makes this a useful reading to do at the midpoint of a long project. The cards that stand in for you will address your needs and how you as an artist have changed since the project began. Maybe you have developed a more emotional connection to the material, and that needs to be incorporated. Maybe you have become more certain of yourself and your skills as time has gone on, and so you need to return to the beginning to bring the early work up to your new higher level.

The cards that represent the project will show you the evolution of the work: if there is harmony or whether it's been a jerky progress. And the transition cards will help you understand how to—and how you did—get from one stage to another.

We start with the past: to go back to your original intentions and who you were when you began the work. Check how the card representing you blends with the card that represents the project. Is there tension? Is one naive, like a Page card or maybe a Seven of Cups, and the other masterful, like the Emperor or a Four of any suit? Do they complement each other? Think back to how you started the work. Was it a sudden flash of inspiration or an idea that slowly evolved? Were you a student at the time, or had you been working for a while? Did you have a firm grasp on the idea, or were you improvising? How do your memories line up with what the cards are saying?

The transition card will move us from past to present. You can read it as representing the work you were doing or maybe the way your personal life changed in the meantime.

Then we get to the present tense. These cards represent you right now and where your project stands. Again, look for complements or stresses, between the past and the present and between you and the project. Switching suits, from Cups to Coins, for example, might mean that where you were once dreamy, now you are dedicated. Going from a Minor Arcana card to a Major Arcana card could mean an increased seriousness on your part. If it's the other way around, from Major to Minor, it could be that your work is evolving from being allegorical to something much more personal and simple.

The next transition card is going to help you figure out what you need to do next. Consider it an "Advice" card. It will tell you how you get from where you stand now to the finished product. If it's a stressful card—say, a Five—you should pay attention to how your process is hindering you. If it's a court card that doesn't seem to be you, there might be an outside voice you need to listen to, so try letting someone else preview the work and get his or her input.

The final section tells us how it will be when it's completed. Do these cards make you happy? Or are you represented by the Tower or something else unpleasant? Remember, this is just the *projected* future that shows the path you are on right *now*. Choose a different approach, and you will see different results. Use any dark cards to rethink your intentions. And let the transition card point out any flaws in your plan.

Look at the reading as a whole. Does it progress naturally? Do the cards work together, or is there a lot of conflict? Does it seem like the cards from the past are stronger than the cards in the future? Maybe there's some idea you had at the beginning that has been abandoned and needs to be reclaimed.

SAMPLE READING

First card: Seven of Coins
Second card: The Star
Third card: Queen of Wands
Fourth card: Two of Cups
Fifth card: The Hierophant
Sixth card: King of Cups
Seventh card: Nine of Swords
Eighth card: Queen of Swords

It's interesting here how many other people are involved. Lots of court cards would suggest that there are collaborators, peers, maybe even romantic partners involved in the project. All of the court cards seem supportive and helpful, so I would advise you to embrace outside opinions and let other people see the work.

In the past, we have the Seven of Coins representing the artist, which would suggest that she is somewhere at the midpoint of her career. At least, this is not the first project she's done. What she's taking on now might be a bit of a change for her, but it's not drastic. She has skills such as patience and discipline, both of which will come in handy. The card that represents the project is the Star, so it'll be something a little quirky. A little *weird*. It might feel more in alignment with what the artist truly wants to do than with her previous output. All in all, these cards have a nice alignment.

The transition card is the Queen of Wands: some sort of outside voice. Maybe the painter recently discovered the work of Leonor Fini, and that had a huge influence on what she wanted to do. Or maybe a mentor looked at what she was doing and gave her the motivation she needed. Whatever the Queen of Wands provided our theoretical artist, it would be an inspirational force.

Now, the artist is in a pretty good place. The Two of Cups suggests there's someone else intimately involved with the project, either as a collaborator or as an assistant, so maybe that Queen of Wands has become a collaborative partner. Or, maybe she's in such a good place in her love life that her romantic partner has become a strong influence on the work. The switch from Coins to Cups means she's working from a much more emotional place, and the evolution from Seven to Two can indicate a new flexibility. It could be less about discipline, working on a set schedule, and more about waiting until the mood strikes.

The Hierophant conflicts a bit with the Star. Where the Star is weird, the Hierophant is traditional. Where the Star is personal, the Hierophant has a social influence. There might be a need for contextualizing her personal experiences within a larger societal pattern. Maybe her story is just another in a long line of similar stories, and she needs to figure that out to give her work more power and to make it more relatable to others.

Here the romantic partner eases the transition from present to future. It's his (or her) input she needs; maybe his story lines up with what she experienced, and realizing that shows her how many others have gone through what she's experienced. The King of Cups is not always the romantic partner, but given that the card lines up so well with the Two of Cups, it seems like an obvious influence.

In the future, we have a dark card for her and a positive card for the project. Both are Swords, so there's a kind of harmony, even if it's a difficult one. Nine of Swords is the card of anxiety. Looking at the cards together, I would think that this Star project requires the artist to plumb some dark parts of her history, because the Star is such a personal card. Lining up with the Hierophant, that dark history would share a societal context. Exploring darker parts of our own history or our country's history can be difficult, and I would guess that is what the Nine of Swords is saying.

But the Queen of Swords provides balance. She is the light in the darkness of the Nine of Swords. She can see through the anxiety to what is real. Having the Queen of Swords as an outcome card for the project is fantastic: it implies a real mastery and control, especially if the project is a book or maybe photography, since Swords rule both. Here I would advise my client to let the project guide her through the darkness; to keep at it until she is able to push through the anxiety and get back on solid ground.

BRINGING YOUR PROJECT INTO THE WORLD

First card: Your project
Second card: Who to ask for help
Third card: What steps do you need to take?
Fourth card: How should you present your project?

Fifth card: The best home for the project
Sixth card: The audience

So you've finished! Congratulations! Now what? This is a reading designed to help a person figure out whether or not a project should be displayed in some way—if it should be made public or kept private. And if it is going to make the long journey into the public eye, what is the best way to go about it?

The first card represents your project in its completed state. This will tell you a lot about what needs to happen. Some cards will indicate that some more work is necessary, although at this stage, that work might need an outside voice. For example, a Five of Wands, the card that asks us to go through yet another round of seemingly endless revisions, might indicate you need someone else to point out the project's weak spots. A card of mastery, such as the Ten of Coins or a King, will tell you that your project is in a state of wholeness and is ready to face an audience.

But the card will also indicate the project's tone and, therefore, how people might react to it. A Wands card is more exciting but less intellectual than a Swords card. And a Major Arcana card such as the Magician means it is less personal to you than a Queen card is. In that particular case, with a Major Arcana card, you should detach yourself from the proceedings and allow other people to see, think, and feel different things for the project than you do. Major Arcana cards are archetypal, and projects represented by Major Arcana will be received as being more archetypal, and the meaning of the work will change for each person who comes in contact with it.

We have four cards that indicate four steps you need to take before you can present this project to an audience. The first card asks us whom we should ask for help. Do we need someone who is nurturing and protective, like the Empress? Or do we need someone with the Ace of Swords: someone able to cut through and assist you ruthlessly in making the project the best it can be?

Don't worry if there is a large divide between the card that represents the project and the card indicating your helper. A conflict here can be useful. An emotional person giving feedback on a work of logic can tell you when you've lost the heart of the work, and so on.

The second card in this row tells you what you need to do. An Eight of Wands would say, "Submit the work to every place you can think of, contact everyone you know, get as many eyes on it as possible." An Ace of Coins would say, "Nurture it slowly, choose where you'd like to go very carefully, and then work steadily to create a space for your work there."

Take this card seriously! Many creatives think their work should stand on its own merits. Sometimes it does, but first you have to make sure you are not the only person who sees that work. If you want an audience, sometimes you have to build your own stage; other times you have to know the right people and make the right contacts. Actually creating the work is one thing; it takes a whole other skill set to present that work to the public, and this card will help you see which skills this project requires of you.

The third card in this row tells you how that work should be presented. This could refer to how you need to present it to the intermediary you're asking to help you, or to the audience itself. Certain cards might indicate that your work is part of a tradition: that there are other artists working in the same genre, and you need to play up that part. Or maybe your work is an Ace: something wildly new descending to the world from the heavens, and its singularity needs to be emphasized. (Of course, it's not *really* that, but it can help sometimes to pretend like it is.)

If you have a cover letter to an agent or gallery owner to write, or a press release or catalog copy, let this card guide your hand. It's particularly helpful because creatives tend to flail a little when they're forced to describe their own work. This will help you get a little perspective and show you how to frame the work for others.

The final card in this row reveals where the work actually belongs. If you've written a book, is it best served by a small publisher that will lavish more attention on it, or by a large publisher that has more power but less individual support? If you're a visual artist, a Ten of Coins might say that you should look to group shows: maybe set up a thematic show with a group of your peers. Remember that this is what best serves the work and not your ego. Of course, all of us would like our work to be placed where we get the most money, the most fame, the most rave reviews and prizes, but not every work needs (or can stand up to) so much attention. Sometimes a delicate touch is needed. And other times you will need to sacrifice your emotional needs for things such as constant feedback or pats on the head for a team that will actually serve your work best.

At the end of the reading, we come to the audience. This is who you will hope to interact with; who is receptive to your work. This card helps you interpret the cards above and will influence strongly how you put the other cards to work.

SAMPLE READING

First card: Queen of Coins
Second card: Five of Wands

Third card: Six of Coins
Fourth card: Five of Cups
Fifth card: Page of Cups
Sixth card: Judgment

The first card indicates that the project is not only complete but regal. Dignified and stable. It's a very strong card to work from, and it requires a lot of hard work. Queens lead with dignity, which is how you should treat your project. It doesn't slump, it doesn't stoop, she remains in control and elite.

But the Queen is also receptive, so she listens to the counsel of the people around her—which is a good match for the Five of Wands that comes up next. This card, representing who you should be asking for help, indicates that the person who can bang your work into its best shape, find all of its weaknesses, and point out any missteps is your closest ally here. The Five of Wands suggests training and learning, so a teacher or mentor, someone who genuinely wants the best for you and is more advanced than you and will see problems that you can't, is key here.

Don't get ruffled by this process. Remember: dignity. This isn't about you, it's about your kingdom, right? The Queen doesn't take it personally when a fire wipes out a segment of her kingdom. She examines the problem and does what needs to be done. Particularly since we are in Coins, and work is not a problem for this Queen. She's practical about all things and can see this process for what it is: something that is going to improve the final product.

The next card, the Six of Coins, shows us what your next task is. The Six of Coins is very interesting here. It says that you need to sort out what and whom you value. You're going to have to ask someone for help, but the person you choose is going to influence what happens to the work once it's out of your hands. For example, if you submitted a piece to a mainstream magazine with a wide audience, it would probably want you to revise the article to fit its style. But if you submit to a smaller, quirkier magazine, the editor there would most likely let you keep more of your signature flourishes. However, that publication would almost certainly pay less. So what do you value? Money and a wide audience? A kind of creative purity? There is no flat right or wrong answer; it will absolutely depend on you and what you feel like you need. It will help you figure that out before you submit the piece. The Six of Coins asks you to stand by your values, which echoes nicely with the dignity of the Queen.

But how should you present the work? The Five of Cups is a dark card, one of disappointment and mourning. I would tell you to pour your heart into it. Establish your deep emotional connection to the work and proceed from there. If the project concerns grief or loss in any way, focus on that.

The final card we have to work with is the Page of Cups, showing us the best home for the work. At some level, the Page of Cups always indicates when we already know the right answer, whether or not we're willing to admit that to ourselves. It comes up sometimes when you've been second-guessing and doubting yourself, even though part of you already knows the correct answer. But it's also another emotional card, a card that says the right home is with someone who really falls in love with your work. It might be someone younger and less experienced than you, in contrast with the mentor card up top. But what's needed here is someone with an emotional connection, someone who will be true to the work.

It's a good combination with the Six of Coins, because the Page shows that in the end, what you should value for this project is the care and attention of the people to whom you entrust it. That what you value is something precious, something that will feel good rather than pay a lot of money. The Queen of Coins is going to be concerned with the financials, of course, but water and earth are a good combination.

The final card shows us the audience, and it is Judgment. It's a kind of rebirth, in that if you have released work into the world in the past, this will mark a new phase. Either a new audience or a new response from that audience. Because the card has to do with karma, the work you put into the project will be the reward you reap, and that makes sense with the Queen of Coins, too.

So when you're making your decisions about what you value, and who will best represent the Page of Cups, or who will help you revise with the Five of Wands, think of this restart. It won't serve you to keep doing the same thing you've always done, or rely on the same audience as before. You need fresh perspectives; you need to value change. Figure out what is different about this work from the works that came before—which could also be part of that Five of Cups card depicting three spilt cups and two upright cups—and see what is new about it. And then make your decisions as if this were a wholly new project; as if you had never created anything before.

CONCLUSION

The more you work with the spreads, the more they will tell you. There are many resources online where you can find other spreads, both traditional and made up by other tarot enthusiasts. I find, though, that the better way to work is to choose a few spreads and stick with them, rather than always trying something new.

Repeated use of the same spreads will help you work more intuitively. Because you don't have to consciously think, "Oh, wait: What was this position supposed to represent again?" you can move directly into looking for patterns, hunting down the story of the reading, and figuring out how the meanings of the cards change based on where they fall in the spread.

Simple repetition is the best thing for learning a new spread until it becomes memorized, automatic, and natural.

HOW TO DO A READING

THE SETUP

First, you'll need a large crystal of smoky quartz and some sage for smudging.

Kidding! I'm only kidding. If you're the type of person who needs a ritualistic setting to really focus, then go for it. Light the candles, put out the crystals, make a circle of salt, whatever you need. But it's not required. You don't need the whole witchy apparatus if the witchy apparatus does not speak to you.

But you'll need to find a place where you can relax. I don't know why this happens, but if I go to a deck of cards when I'm distressed or really anxious, then I pull all the doomsday cards: Ten of Swords, Three of Swords, the Tower, the Devil, Five of Cups—the works. Which certainly does not help with the anxiety.

Next, choose the spread you want to do. Are things complicated enough that you want a Celtic Cross, which is just loaded with information and patterns, or do you want a quick hit of Past-Present-Future three-card draw? Or do you just want to ask individual questions and pull one card for each answer? There's no wrong way to pull cards, but it helps if you have a clear intention ahead of time.

Get comfortable. Rather than focusing on the problem, which I find just causes a kind of mental fixation and stubbornness, clear your mind. It helps to approach the deck and what is about to transpire with a kind of lightness. Think of all the people who love you and whom you love. Feel gratitude for their existence. And while you're doing that, shuffle the cards. You can either have a preset method of shuffling—personally, I prefer three shuffles and three cuts—or you can just smear the cards around on the floor until they feel right.

Remember: this is not about foretelling the future, this is about uncovering what you already know. That knowledge will help you deal with pulling dark cards or maybe getting answers you don't like. If you are too invested in the answers, it's easier to dismiss anything that feels difficult, even if it's something that you do really need to hear. So be open. Be flexible. And then anoint yourself in rosemary oil.

Kidding again! Then pull some cards and let's see how to figure out what they're saying.

GET TO KNOW THE CARDS

First, you need to have an intimate knowledge of the cards. This part takes awhile.

There is the surface definition of the card, the one that comes with the little paper manual shoved into the box with your deck. You know, the "Queen of Coins is a Taurus, Virgo, or Capricorn woman" stuff. These explanations are handy when you're just getting started; they give you a kind of baseline understanding of the cards. But the more nuanced your understanding of the cards becomes, the more helpful they will become to you.

The first thing you'll want to do when you are learning the tarot is to draw one card every morning. Let it represent your day ahead. I still do this, actually. If you have to remind yourself what the card means, then refer back to the card definitions here or in another guide. Maybe search for information about the card online; get some differing opinions.

Next, look at the artwork. Notice the colors, the feel of the card. Take note of the number of the card, if it's not a court card. If it is a court card, ask yourself if the person depicted reminds you of anyone in your life.

Then go about your day, but keep the card in your mind. Refer back to it from time to time—you can carry it in your pocket or put it up someplace where you can see it if you like. What happens during the day that reminds you of the card? Do you have a conversation that goes the way the card might suggest? Do you meet someone who reminds you of the card? Is there a pattern to your day—something that keeps happening, or a feeling that keeps emerging? Thinking about these things will bring a more expansive meaning to the cards. You'll see how many different moods, behaviors, and circumstances these cards can indicate.

Let's say you draw the Nine of Wands for your first day. If you read the manual, it will tell you that this card represents "defensiveness." During the day, you find yourself walking down the street, and you start to attract some unwanted attention. You can stiffen, your head might go down, you might grab the strap on your purse. That can be a feeling for the Nine of Wands.

Later, you'll get into work, and that coworker who is always driving you mad starts to take credit for an idea that was actually yours. You stand your ground and confront him about it. That can be a Nine of Wands.

After work, it's been a trying day, and you're invited out with some coworkers or maybe some friends. Instead of talking about your feelings, maybe you let your shyness take over, and you kind of shrink back into yourself. It makes you feel lonely, even within a crowd. That's also the Nine of Wands.

So you can see how many different situations can be a Nine of Wands situation. These situations become significant because you're putting this added attention on them. This helps you understand your cards better, but it also helps you understand patterns in your behavior better. So later, when you pull the Nine of Wands again, you understand that you should pay attention to all of the ways you become defensive in a bad way—shutting down in social situations, thereby preventing you from making new friends and connecting with others—and how you act defensively in a good way, such as standing up for yourself when you are disrespected at work.

Try to avoid predicting how you think a day will go based on the card you pull. This is more about drawing your attention to patterns rather than giving you a glimpse of the future. As in, don't assume that just because you pull the Lovers you are going to meet the love of your life today. But pay attention to what does happen, because that will expand your understanding of that card. And don't assume that because you pull the Tower you are going to experience a total breakdown or you're going to be hit by a car. Maybe it is only acknowledging difficult times you're already going through rather than indicating that you are in for even more. I've pulled the Tower and felt the dread of "Oh no, what now?" but then experienced it as a movie that moved me to cry. (In that particular instance, it was really crazy crying, too: the "I hope my face doesn't fall off" kind of crying, so it seemed only right to get the Tower that day.)

Once you've done this daily draw for a while, perhaps consider drawing two cards. That will help you understand how cards interact with one another; how one influences the meaning of the other.

The point of this, besides familiarizing you with the cards, is to see how the cards change meaning out in the world, rather than just in a closed-room, trying-to-get-answers kind of way. It's important to understand how many times we walk through the situations depicted on the cards rather than understanding their rote definition. That will give them more meaning.

CHOOSE A DECK

It's important to find a deck that feels right to you. The artwork on each deck is different, and some even change the names of the suits, the order of the cards, the names of the figures. What is the King in one deck will be the Father in another. Justice is sometimes number eleven, sometimes number eight. None of this really matters as long as the deck resonates with you.

It's easiest to learn the basics on a standard deck. The Rider-Waite-Smith is a good option because it is the standard from which most contemporary decks work. But there are plenty of beautiful, unique decks, from the Minchiate, to the Morgan-Greer, to the Golden.

FIND THE PATTERNS

First you'll need to select a spread that suits your question. It can be one of the spreads included here in this book, one that you've learned elsewhere, or one of your own devising. It doesn't matter for this lesson.

Take a look at the cards and see what repeats. Is there one particular suit that dominates? Are there mostly cards from the Major Arcana or mostly cards from the Minor Arcana? Are there a lot of court cards? Is there one color that keeps popping up? How does that color resonate with you?

Let's take these questions first, and then we'll talk about numbers. We now know what each suit means, but what does it mean when there are a lot of Swords cards but no Cups cards? Or vice versa? Here is what it means when one suit outnumbers the others:

Swords

Swords represent thought and how that thought is expressed. When you have a lot of Swords, there is a lot of thinking involved. Swords is the only suit where the more Swords cards that show up, the more difficult the circumstances are, and so a reading that is heavy on Swords can be like a mind cluttered with too many thoughts: a mind that is eaten up with obsessive thinking and anxiety. This is not always true, of course. Swords also represent writing, and so it's possible that the difficulty lies only in getting your thoughts across on the page or to someone else. But in general, if you have a lot of Swords, there are a lot of quandaries, and it could be that thinking your way through your problems is not helping you. Look to see where the Swords are positioned to tell you whether or not they are useful.

If your reading is light on Swords or missing them entirely: It could be that you are relying too heavily on the other aspects—emotion, excitement, work—and not enough on your mind.

Cups

Cups represent your emotional life, which includes love and connection to others. There are dark Cups cards—the five, the seven (sometimes), the eight—and so look to see first if the Cups cards included are dark or light. If dark, so many Cups can mean you are feeling overwhelmed by your emotions, that you are so controlled by your feelings that you are not thinking logically, or that you can't find stability because you are letting your feelings guide you rather than following a plan. But if the cards are bright, then it merely means that you should be letting your intuition guide you right now; that your emotions are the markers you should be following. But either way, too many Cups can feel like too much water—like you are splashing around and can't quite touch the bottom with your toes.

If your reading is light on Cups or missing them entirely: Your feelings or your romantic life should be set aside for now, and let other parts of your life take the focus.

Wands

Too much of any suit can be overwhelming, but too many Wands cards is particularly prone to burnout. Fire is also difficult to translate into the real world, in the sense that it needs another suit to ground it, or else it has a tendency to sputter. Too much excitement, without anything to give it form, can feel like that one-too-many cups of coffee. You're all hopped up but too jittery to actually function, and now you've got an upset stomach to boot. So wands are best tempered by another suit, and it might be up to you to compensate to make sure that energy has somewhere to go.

If your reading is light on Wands or missing them entirely: Have you been feeling tired lately, or uninspired? Your excitement might be drained, but it might be time to look at the task ahead as a duty, and let the spark be nourished again afterward.

Coins

Because the Coins signify the earth element, too many Coins cards can begin to feel like depression. It's that weight of responsibility that can feel like rocks piled on top of your body. It can also signify an overemphasis on the material side of life, from money to your belongings, and that sense of possessiveness can spill over into inappropriate areas of your life, like with your lover or your friends. It might be time to relax and let go a bit. Even if times are tough and require a lot of work and a serious attitude, try to find some lightness where you can.

If your reading is light on Coins or missing them entirely: Without Coins, it can be difficult to make real changes or turn an idea into reality. There is a time for daydreaming, but a lack of Coins cards can indicate that an inadequate work ethic might be hindering you.

When it comes to Major versus Minor Arcana, a lot of Major Arcana cards can mean that what you're going through right now has a kind of heightened importance. You're working with big energy, and that can be overwhelming. You're not just piddling around with the Two of Wands, you're dealing with the Magician and so on. It can be said that you have more options with the Minor Arcana than with the Major. Different ways to do things, and you can choose the best way to respond to the situation depicted in the card. With the Major Arcana, it's almost as if you can't squirm away. One must deal with the situation at hand, and that situation will deal with you any way it pleases.

But when you're heavy on Minor Arcana, it can feel almost like you have too many options. You can choose to do things any way you like, so how can you ever know which thing to choose? Freedom can feel like anxiety! It can feel truly frustrating when you go to the cards for guidance about what to do, and the cards come back to you with, "I don't care, do whatever you want." If that's the case, write down your thoughts about the reading, carry it around with you for a while and see if things become clearer with reflection. And if not, feel free to shrug and deal out another spread of cards.

Numbers

The numbers of the cards are as significant as the suits of the Minor Arcana. Getting several cards of the same number, then, is something that also needs to be examined. Before each number in the card descriptions, I added a description of the basic meaning of each number. If you don't remember their meanings off the top of your head, you might want to go back and refamiliarize yourself with them.

Note that the Major Arcana cards are numbered as well; it's not just the Minor Arcana. And so the One of the Magician corresponds with the Aces, the High Priestess corresponds with the

Twos, and so on. The cards of the Major Arcana that are higher than ten correspond with the digit that is at the end of their number. For example, the Moon is at thirteen, so it belongs next to the Empress and also the Threes.

To see how this functions in a reading, let's look at a group of Five cards: the Hierophant, the Devil, Five of Swords, Five of Cups, Five of Wands, and Five of Coins.

If you have several Five cards in one reading, then you have my sympathies. These are not easy cards to deal with. The Hierophant sets the stage for the Five. He is the ideal Five, the only one of the cards that isn't a little bit scary. So we need to look at why that is.

The Hierophant, if you remember, is a perfectly balanced person. The four elements of the deck—Swords (intellect), Cups (emotion), Fire (passion or spirit), Coins (practicality)—are combined with the fifth element: spirit. The Hierophant then uses his powers for the greater good. He is a leader, which is why this is a card of the higher self.

But if that Five becomes imbalanced, then there is trouble. If he uses his power for ego gratification rather than to help others, then he tips over into being the Devil. If he emphasizes his intellect too much, he can become cruel, and so he tips into the Five of Swords. If he overemphasizes his emotions, he can be disappointed, and so he tips into the Five of Cups. And so on.

If you have a reading with three or four Five cards then, even if one of those cards is not the Hierophant, he becomes key to the reading. The Hierophant becomes the way out of the difficult situation you've constructed. If you rebalance yourself, go back to working for the greater good. Then you can find your way through the difficult Five cards you've drawn.

It works this way for all of the numbers. The Three of the Empress is the highest version of that group: she is emotional, but she uses those emotions to fuel her creativity. With the Moon, the number thirteen, you are rather at the mercy of your emotions. They are not useful to you because they are overpowering you and turning into fear. With the Three of Wands, she's relying on her love of adventure to inspire her. And so it goes down the line, from one to ten.

The only two cards this does not relate to is the Fool, which is represented by either no number or the number zero, and the World. Both stand outside this system, the Fool meaning beginning and the World representing ending or completion.

All of this must seem like so much information to remember! It *is* a lot. But the more you read, the more all of this becomes natural and intuitive. Soon you'll be scanning the reading, and, without even counting up the different numbers, you'll have a good sense of the tone.

And if you forget to check all of this every reading, don't worry. Pick up as much as you can now without feeling overwhelmed or bogged down. As it becomes more natural to you, then you can get more intricate with the patterns.

TELL A STORY

Let's start with a simple reading, like Past Present Future. First, decide what it is you want to ask. If you are reading for yourself, try to formulate a question about your predicament. There is obviously going to be a lot of information, a big swirl of ideas and feelings and experiences you've had about this topic, but try to narrow it down to one question. That will help you figure out how the cards relate.

Let's say that you want to ask, "What is going on in my relationship?" You know your own history, with all of its ups and downs, all of its fogginess and uncertainties, but for now, we want to try to set aside as much of that as possible, so we can find a new story to tell ourselves.

The reason we do this is to interrupt the current narrative in your head. If you've reached a crisis point in your relationship or your job or your family life, it might be that the story you are telling yourself about your situation has stopped being helpful to you. Think about it: we construct stories about what happens to us all of the time. We come up with stories to tell other people about what is going on with us, and we tell ourselves those same stories. If those stories become too rooted in a negative image we have of ourselves, or just flat-out do not reflect reality, or clash with someone else's version of events, then we can get stuck in that story. And it's not serving us.

For example, a person whose significant other has left her for someone else might tell herself this story: "I have been betrayed, things were wonderful before that other person wormed her way in," and so on. Instead of maybe what truly happened: you were drifting apart, the relationship had been sour for a long time, and you were not happy, either.

So the tarot reading tells us another story, and that story gives us insight into a different version of events. It can be a little like therapy, sure. (And this is where I put in the disclaimer that if you are suffering from depression or anxiety, you should certainly seek professional help from a therapist or a doctor and not a deck of cards.) The question you come up with in the beginning is going to be the setup for the story. The cards will fill in the plot points, the characters, and so on.

Shuffle the cards and lay them out however you wish. If a card is upside down, you can decide if you want to read it that way or if you prefer to turn it around. Some tarot readers see an upside-down card—a "reversed" card—as meaning the opposite of its given definition. Others think you've overcome the situation in the card, while others see it as a task that you need to complete in order to turn the card right side up. Still others think it's a combination of all of these. You are free to interpret a reversed card any way you like, or disregard its reversed position and simply turn it back around.

Take note of any patterns; for instance, one suit shows up more than once, or a number repeats, or a mostly Major or Minor Arcana presence. If there are court cards, see if they remind you of someone. If you're asking about love, is your partner in the cards? And if so, is he or she represented by the Page, the Knight, the Queen, or the King, or maybe one of the Major Arcana? And if your partner isn't in the cards, does that feel significant to you? Does that mean the problem lies outside of what he or she might be doing?

You've taken note of the patterns and the imagery. If any card seems a bit foggy to you, read up on the meaning of the card and see if that helps. Now it's time for you to tell a story.

This is an intuitive act, and so the way you do it will be different from the way I do it or from how the person down the street does it. And that's fine. You will want to experiment a bit to find the way that feels natural to you. Me, I talk out loud. I don't know why it helps, but it does. I start telling myself the story out loud as if I were reading a book, and I'm sure my neighbors have alerted the authorities about me by now. ("She talks to herself! All the time! We're concerned!") Others might write down the story or jot down notes that come to mind while looking at the cards.

A three-card draw is a good place to start because it has a very obvious beginning, middle, and end. So take what you know of the cards and tell yourself a story about them. Say you draw the Knight of Cups, Three of Swords, and Six of Cups. We go from a romantic but not very serious figure, to the card of heartache and betrayal, but we have a bit of a happy ending with pleasure and friendship. Here the story is obvious, but it's up to you to figure out how it relates to your own situation. The Knight of Cups is more interested in the chase than in a real relationship: Was that the person who broke your heart, or was that you? Were you really committed to this person? With the Three of Swords, it can sometimes mean a really old hurt, stemming from something in your childhood. Are you really upset that the relationship is over, or did it just bring up abandonment issues? And how do you reintroduce the pleasure of the future into your life? Dating, or do you just want to spend more time with friends right now?

The cards are the skeleton, and your task in the reading is to flesh it out into something real and full.

HOW TO READ FOR SOMEONE ELSE

Many tarot card readers find it much easier to read for someone else than to read their own cards. Unless we are trying to read for our romantic partners—not really a good idea, by the way—we can remain more detached and less invested in a good result. If you've been struggling to read for yourself, you might be surprised how satisfying it can be to read for another person. It's a productive way to learn.

So if you're still a beginner with the tarot, find someone who

won't mind you, um, experimenting on him or her a little. M
sure the person knows you're new to this, and don't feel shy ret__
ring back to the basic card definitions if you've forgotten some.

The process is essentially the same, except that you let the person you are reading for formulate the question. Don't ask for too
much information, or it'll ping your confirmation bias during the
reading. You can put too much emphasis on the cards that relate
directly to his or her version of events. Part of that can be because
you're worried it'll be embarrassing if the person you are reading for
says, "Actually, that's not how it is at all." Remember that messing
up and getting things wrong is an important part of every learning
process! But also because sometimes, with the people we care for,
we can want to look for good things to tell them.

Which brings me to the next point: don't be afraid to deliver bad
news. I don't mean that if your friend gets the Tower you should
say, "Oh yeah, you're screwed." Ask her a lot of questions. "The
Tower generally indicates a lot of tumult; is there something you're
going through?" Don't assume, if you're reading for someone you
know, that you know the entirety of her situation. Let the person
fill in the blanks. If there's a court card, ask, "Who do you think
this represents?" If the card doesn't remind her of anyone in her
life, ask if there is a part of her life that this card might represent.

You are here to tell a story, in its outline form. But when you are
reading for someone else, instead of you filling in the details, she's
going to do that. So take it step by step, card by card, checking
in with the person at every point along the way to make sure you
haven't wandered far into the weeds, and ask for constant feedback.

KEEP A JOURNAL

This is most important when you're just starting out, but I still find it helpful today, years after my own learning process. When you do a reading for yourself, write down the structure of the spread and your notes about what you think the reading meant. Then, as your situation changes and develops, check back in with the reading and see if the meaning changes for you; if things are progressing the way you'd predicted.

This will also help you see patterns in your own readings. Certain cards can take on special meanings for you, outside of their traditional meanings. When the Three of Coins shows up, you can instantly click with the pattern: "Oh, whenever that shows up, it means I should be focusing more on this project over here." Or "Whenever the Seven of Cups shows up, my ex-boyfriend the liar starts emailing me again." Of course, it won't be true every time, but keeping a journal, and seeing your own patterns and repetitions, will help you develop a more personal relationship with your deck.

AND THERE WE HAVE IT!

You now have all you need to know to let the tarot guide you through your artistic process. You've learned the meaning of the cards, some spreads to help with the complications that have arisen, and you have learned the best way to do a reading. Hopefully, you have also picked up along the way some inspiration from the stories of how other artists work.

CONCLUSION

You'll find that the tarot can be an endless source of inspiration. It can get you through blocks, help you manage your time, focus your attention on the most pressing matters, and even tell you when you're done. It all depends on how you work it.

Remember that creation is always an act of optimism. To take an empty space and then try to build something there—something beautiful, something new—takes courage. It takes courage to devote yourself to something as unpredictable, difficult, time consuming, and *life* consuming as art. You are beginning a process that might take years before you see results, that will eat up your time and energy, and that will, in many ways, change your life. That courage should not be disregarded.

You will have to quell doubt along the way: your own and others'. You'll have to face down disappointment and frustration. There will be days when you feel like nothing is working, and there will be days when everything is flowing so smoothly it will be effortless. And after one of those days, you'll wake up the next morning and find that feeling eludes you again; that you essentially have to start all over again.

You know that thing people say about how once you do the thing you're supposed to be doing, the universe will meet you halfway? All of that follow-your-bliss stuff? Crazy nonsense! If that were true, every artist would have been celebrated in his lifetime, would have lived in perfect mental health, and would have conquered his demons without the help of alcohol or drug abuse. It's hard to go down deep into your psyche and mess around with what you find there, and then to take that chaos and try to turn it into something beautiful and useful.

So don't be discouraged by setbacks. Don't think that because something is hard it is not worth doing. Something being difficult is the sign that it *is* worth doing. Because if it were easy, if we were showered with rewards for doing it, if the universe did start paying our rent and gifting us with free child care to give us the time and space to do what we needed to do, then everyone would do it.

Are you determined? You bought a book about creativity, so you must be determined. Are you ready? You read the whole book—and I can be pretty long-winded!—so you must be ready. Keep in mind that the best time to start something is always now. Not "After this episode of *The Wire* is over." Not "Tomorrow when I am not so tired." Not "After I finish reading every book on the subject," "After I learn ten new languages," "After I become a super-perfect genius and awesome." It's now, when the impulse strikes.

And that's how the tarot can help you.

Look at starting a new artistic project as beginning a big adventure. You're not just off to summit a mountain, you are actually *building* it. Think about the supplies you'll need, such as the maps and the surveying equipment. You'll probably forget something. That's okay: you can just go back and fetch it when you need it. Think about how long you think it might take. Then *double* that amount, and not until you have reached that second, longer amount of time are you allowed to even slightly scold yourself or doubt yourself about how long this is taking.

And every time you look at the map questioningly, every time you wonder what the hell you're doing, whether you are actually in the Andes when you thought you were in the Carpathians, you can ask the tarot to nudge you in the right direction. Every time the story you've been telling yourself about what you're doing and why seems inadequate, the tarot can help you update it.

And hell, if that doesn't work—if the cards aren't making sense, and things have broken down a bit—come find me online or in real life. I'll be happy to help you out.

Remember to drink plenty of water. Remember to eat fruit, get enough sleep, feed yourself with things that are beautiful and helpful to you. Remember always to be learning, to humble yourself enough until you know that you can never really know enough, that you will always be a student. Remember to protect your work from the people who will attack you for doing it, just because they can.

Remember that you are courageous and that your heart is true. And that what you are doing now is important. Remember that we are on the planet to learn and grow and take care of one another, and making something beautiful is a way of taking care of others.

What happens next is up to you.